Global Women Leaders

NEW HORIZONS IN LEADERSHIP STUDIES

Series Editor: Joanne B. Ciulla, *Academic Director, Institute for Ethical Leadership and Professor of Leadership Ethics, Department of Management and Global Business, Rutgers Business School, USA*

This important series is designed to make a significant contribution to the development of leadership studies. This field has expanded dramatically in recent years and the series provides an invaluable forum for the publication of high quality works of scholarship and shows the diversity of leadership issues and practices around the world.

The main emphasis of the series is on the development and application of new and original ideas in leadership studies. It pays particular attention to leadership in business, economics and public policy and incorporates the wide range of disciplines which are now part of the field. Global in its approach, it includes some of the best theoretical and empirical work with contributions to fundamental principles, rigorous evaluations of existing concepts and competing theories, historical surveys and future visions.

Titles in the series include:

Poor Leadership and Bad Governance
Reassessing Presidents and Prime Ministers in North America, Europe and Japan
Edited by Ludger Helms

Leadership by Resentment
From *Ressentiment* to Redemption
Ruth Capriles

Critical Perspectives on Leadership
Emotion, Toxicity, and Dysfunction
Edited by Jeanette Lemmergaard and Sara Louise Muhr

Authentic Leadership
Clashes, Convergences and Coalescences
Edited by Donna Ladkin and Chellie Spiller

Leadership and Transformative Ambition in International Relations
Mark Menaldo

Extreme Leadership
Leaders, Teams and Situations Outside the Norm
Edited by Cristina M. Giannantonio and Amy Hurley-Hanson

Community as Leadership
Gareth Edwards

Madness and Leadership
From Antiquity to the New Common Era
Savvas Papacostas

The Leadership Imagination
An Introduction to Taxonomic Leadership Analysis
Donald R. LaMagdeleine

Thinking Differently about Leadership
A Critical History of Leadership Studies
Suze Wilson

Politics, Ethics and Change
The Legacy of James MacGregor Burns
Edited by George R. Goethals and Douglas Bradburn

Global Women Leaders
Breaking Boundaries
Regina Wentzel Wolfe and Patricia H. Werhane

Global Women Leaders

Breaking Boundaries

Regina Wentzel Wolfe

Professor, Catholic Theological Union, USA

Patricia H. Werhane

Professor Emerita, DePaul University and Professor Emerita, University of Virginia, USA

NEW HORIZONS IN LEADERSHIP STUDIES

Cheltenham, UK • Northampton, MA, USA

© Regina Wentzel Wolfe and Patricia H. Werhane 2017

All rights reserved. No part of this publication may be reproduced, stored in a retrieval system or transmitted in any form or by any means, electronic, mechanical or photocopying, recording, or otherwise without the prior permission of the publisher.

Published by
Edward Elgar Publishing Limited
The Lypiatts
15 Lansdown Road
Cheltenham
Glos GL50 2JA
UK

Edward Elgar Publishing, Inc.
William Pratt House
9 Dewey Court
Northampton
Massachusetts 01060
USA

Paperback edition 2018

A catalogue record for this book
is available from the British Library

Library of Congress Control Number: 2017947091

This book is available electronically in the Elgaronline
Business subject collection
DOI 10.4337/9781785368714

Printed on elemental chlorine free (ECF)
recycled paper containing 30% Post-Consumer Waste

ISBN 978 1 78536 870 7 (cased)
ISBN 978 1 78536 871 4 (eBook)
ISBN 978 1 78811 336 6 (paperback)

Typeset by Columns Design XML Ltd, Reading
Printed and bound in the USA

To our daughters

Cathleen, Hillary, Kelly (deceased), Maria, Marijke and Stephanie

Contents

Preface ix

Introduction 1

PART I INDIAN WOMEN LEADERS

Introduction: The Indian context 15

1 Jeroo Billimoria: Social entrepreneur 20
2 Astrid Lobo Gajiwala, Ph.D.: Head, Tata Memorial Hospital Tissue Bank 25
3 Corinne Kumar: International Coordinator and Founder, World Courts of Women 35
4 Sharma Sujata, Ph.D.: Director, Tapan Rehabilitation Society 43

PART II JAPANESE WOMEN LEADERS

Introduction: The Japanese context 49

5 Hisa Anan: Independent Director, Megmilk Snow Brand Co., Ltd. 52
6 Nobuko Hiwasa: Retired Independent Director, Megmilk Snow Brand Co., Ltd. 56
7 Yukako Kurose: General Manager, CSR Planning Office, Teijin Ltd. 66
8 Ryoko Nagata: Senior Vice President, Japan Tobacco Inc. 68
9 Mieko Yoshida: Retired Executive Officer and General Manager of Quality Assurance Department, R&D and Quality Assurance Division, Nisshin Seifun Group Inc. 74

PART III JORDANIAN WOMEN LEADERS

Introduction: The Jordanian context 81

10 Jumana Ghunaimat: Editor-in-Chief, *Al Ghad* Newspaper 87
11 Reem Abu Hassan, JD: Attorney at Law 92
12 Nadia Shamroukh: Chairwoman, Jordanian Women's Union 98

PART IV UNITED KINGDOM WOMEN LEADERS

Introduction: The United Kingdom context 107

13 Terrie Alafat, CBE: Chief Executive, Chartered Institute of Housing 113
14 Claire Jenkins: Non-Executive Director, Sports Direct International plc 124
15 Francesca Raleigh O'Connell: Founder, SculptureLondon 137
16 Professor Catherine Peckham, CBE, MD, FMedSci: Professor of Paediatric Epidemiology, University College London 146

Conclusion 153

Bibliography 157
Index 181

Preface

We present a collection of essays on global women leaders in business, nonprofit organizations and government. They have risen to positions that many young women today aspire to achieve. While there is literature lauding American women leaders, there is less emphasis on non-North American women who hold leadership positions. Yet today, as young women are accepting positions in global organizations, they need to be aware of these fascinating women who can serve as role models for those joining local and global enterprises.

A recent study of North American women business leaders found that the women shared some common characteristics. They were, not surprisingly, smart, self-confident and determined to succeed. They dismissed or ignored what might seem to be discriminatory challenges because of their gender. Most of the women were situational leaders, adapting and readapting themselves to new situations and challenging circumstances. The women had a less hierarchical style than often evidenced in corporate leadership. They were more collaborative, unafraid of hiring their successors, and viewed leadership as an ongoing process that focused on improving organizational performance, not merely their own personal careers (Werhane et al., 2007).

As Nancy Adler put it some time ago:

> The CEO of a global company cannot change her message for each of the countries and cultures in which her company operates. Global leaders, unlike domestic leaders, address people worldwide ... a fundamental distinction is that global leadership is neither domestic nor multi-domestic: It focuses on cross-cultural interaction. Thus global leaders must articulate and communicate a vision which, in and of itself is global ... and compelling to people from around the world (Adler, 1997, 175).

These are all characteristics of women in the North American study. We wondered if we would find similar characteristics in women leaders from other countries. Interestingly, there are more than a few women leaders today in what may seem to be unlikely locations. We have recently interviewed five leading Japanese women and three Jordanians. We have also had opportunities to interview women leaders in India and the United Kingdom. This book, which tells the stories of these women, is intended for practitioners as well as academics who work in the leadership field. We want to thank all the women for agreeing to participate in this endeavor. We also want to thank Nobuko Hiwasa for introducing us to Japanese business leaders and Reem Abu Hassan for introducing us to Jordanian women leaders. We also want to thank Nicola Pleas and Manjit Monga for introductions to some outstanding women in India, and Olga Basirov, Maurine Murtaugh and Rosanna Peeling for introducing some outstanding women from the United Kingdom to our project. Finally, we want to thank Caroline Scullin for sharing her expertise in strategic communications.

Each woman we feature tells her story differently. Some have just allowed us to record their narratives; others have responded to questions to tell their stories. Each story is unique; each tells of a journey, not yet complete, that opens up a perspective on leadership in global political economies.

This book is aimed at a wide variety of readers – men and women students and faculty in academia, men and women in the workforce, men and women who are entrepreneurs, who engage in social ventures, and who work in government organizations. We hope that the stories of and insights from the women we feature will resonate with this wide audience. We thank Edward Elgar Publishers and their editors for encouraging us to write this book, with particular thanks to Karissa Venne and Michaela Doyle for their editorial assistance in guiding the project and Melanie Marshall for her copyediting skills. Finally, we thank all the women we featured in this volume for allowing us to include them.

Introduction

For decades, there has been an insistence that the world needs women leaders. Although progress has been made, across the globe the number of women in senior leadership positions in business, government and nonprofit sectors remains disproportionately low. This collection of essays presents the stories of successful women leaders in India, Japan, Jordan and the United Kingdom.

The slow progress of women's advancement was repeatedly noted in many of the reports that were issued in 2015 to mark both the twentieth anniversary of the Beijing Platform for Action (BPfA) and the deadline for achieving the Millennium Development Goals (MDGs), many of which focused on women's empowerment. The research findings point to mixed results of achieving that empowerment.

One of the high points is the increasing number of girls being educated, more than ever before. However, there is little evidence that successes on the educational front translate into successes in addressing the gender gap in workplace participation in general or, more particularly, in increasing the number of women in the ranks of the most senior leaders in major global organizations. In the 20 years since BPfA, 'the chances for women to participate in the labour market remain almost 27 percentage points lower than those for men' (Debusscher, 2015). In addition, there has been little change in sectoral and occupational segregation and a persistent gender wage gap. International Labour Organization (ILO) reports indicate a bit of progress in women's advancement through the 'glass ceiling' with some women even being appointed to C-suite and/or board positions. Overall, however, 'while women have advanced in business and management, they continue to be shut out of higher level economic decision-making despite activism in the last decade to smash the "glass ceiling"' (ILO, 2015). The progress of women is described as 'glacial.'

1

In its 2016 report surveying 36 countries, Grant Thornton International found on average women hold 24 percent of senior positions in business. This is a return to a previous high from a downturn in 2015. However, the number of firms in which there are no women in senior positions remains unchanged at 33 percent. Eastern European and Asian countries continue to top the list of countries with women in senior leadership positions at 35 percent and 34 percent respectively; Russia leads with 45 percent and is followed by Lithuania and the Philippines both at 39 percent. It is interesting to note that in Eastern Europe the rate is attributed to the old communist 'maxim that men and women are equal partners [which] seems to have sparked a trend within the business world that shows little sign of diminishing' (Grant Thornton International Ltd., 2016). The five ASEAN countries included in the Grant Thornton study all rank above the global average in terms of the number of women who are in senior leadership positions. This is attributed in part to social and governmental support for women's education, with large numbers of women completing degrees at both the undergraduate and graduate level, sometimes in larger numbers than men.

The findings are less promising when it comes to Japan, India, the United Kingdom and Jordan, the four countries in which the women in this study work. These countries have consistently been below the global average when it comes to the number of women in senior management positions. Japan at 7 percent is at the bottom of the list; India at 16 percent and the United Kingdom at 21 percent are in the bottom third (Grant Thornton, 2016). Jordan, a country not included in the Grant Thornton study, ties the United Kingdom at 21 percent according to data prepared by the International Finance Corporation (2015).

WOMEN AND LEADERSHIP

One of the most controversial issues in studying women leaders is the question: Do women lead differently? In order to explore that question, in the section below we briefly outline some traditional theories of leadership. This will be useful in considering whether one can distinguish certain qualities that differentiate women leaders from their male counterparts. This discussion will also provide a lens through which to consider the women leaders featured in this volume.

Are Men and Women Different?

There is literature that argues that there are certain traits, presumably inherited traits, which distinguish leaders from the rest of us. According to this theory, leaders are born with these character traits. These vary in the literature, but the most commonly cited innate traits are intelligence, self-confidence, determination or drive to succeed, integrity and sociability (Shriberg and Shriberg, 2011). Some theorists add charisma to the list (Conger and Kanungo, 1998). Being tall has also been cited as an important trait of leadership although there is only weak evidence that this is important.

If trait theory has any validity, then do women have genetically different leadership traits than men? Whether or not such so-called traits are genetic has never been proven, and it is difficult at best to identify leaders by these traits when they are children or young adults. Of course, one can socially construct and reinterpret these qualities of leadership after the fact when they have become leaders through appealing to these so-called traits as descriptive of certain leaders.

The issue remains, however, as to whether and in what ways men are different from women and how those differences might affect their leadership styles. Early in the twentieth century none other than Sigmund Freud argued, 'I cannot evade the notion ... that for women the level of what is ethically normal is different from what it is in men' (Freud, 1925; 1961, 257, re-quoted in Gilligan, 1977 in Ciulla et al., 2013, volume 2, 286).

One distinguished contemporary thinker, Carol Gilligan, argues that there are vast differences between men and women. Whether or not these are genetic traits is a question Gilligan does not consider. Rather, she argues that 'the feminine experience and construction of social reality [is in a] distinctive voice, recognizable in the different perspective [the voice] brings to bear on the construction and resolution of moral problems' (Gilligan, 1997 in Ciulla et al., 2013, volume 2, 286). In other words, women perceive and frame their experiences using socially constructed mindsets or mental models that are distinctive for women. Gilligan argues that women are less individualistic and less self-absorbed than men, are extremely concerned about their relationships with others, contextualize rather than generalize moral problems, make moral judgments that are situational rather than universal, and exhibit a model of leadership that is collaborative rather than hierarchically focused. Gilligan backs up these contentions with a series of empirical studies of women decision-makers who seem to demonstrate the validity of her claims. For example, Gilligan found that most women identify morality as situational, but she also found an overall consensus that inflicting gratuitous harm on other people is almost always wrong. A feeling of the value and moral importance of empathy and fellow feeling usually overrode questions of fairness or justice. Women also worried about their own sense of self-identity and whether they were respected as independent individuals with the capacity to make their own decisions. Taking responsibility for their choices was not an issue, but women often worried about whether they were taken seriously by others, particularly men, as morally equal beings. She found:

> Women impose a distinctive construction on moral problems ... The development of women's moral judgment appears to proceed from an initial concern with survival, to a focus on goodness, [identified primarily as avoiding harm to others,] and finally to a principled understanding of nonviolence as the most adequate guide to the just resolution of moral conflicts (Gilligan, 1977 in Ciulla et al., 2013, volume 2, 304).

If Gilligan is even partly correct, then women leaders will socially construct reality differently than men, being less egoistical, more relationship focused, and more collaborative as leaders than their male counterparts. Such generalizations are not absolute, and many men also exhibit these allegedly female leadership characteristics. Alternately, women as a gendered group might also socially construct their ideas of leadership from a masculine point of view, and some do. What we can conclude is that how a person constructs a definition of leadership frames her own leadership style and the ways in which she interprets the leadership capabilities of others.

Leadership Styles

Carol Gilligan's studies were conducted in the 1970s. Nevertheless, they set up a stereotype for women and women leaders that exists in the literature today. This stereotype, recently evidenced in another study of American women leaders (Werhane et al., 2007), found that women leaders are more likely than men to be transformational leaders. A transformational leader is a leader who sees her role as inspiring her followers and her organization with a set of goals or a vision, goals that together the organization and its constituents all agree to and contribute to achieving those ends (Bass, 1998; Burns, 2003). It is not a top-down hierarchical model because rather than ordering the pursuit of goals or vision, the leader convinces and inspires followers thereby bringing them along in pursuit of shared goals or visions.

According to this same study, women were less likely to emulate a model of a transactional leader. A transactional leader is a person who, because of her position, has authority over others, sees herself in charge and views leader-follower relationships as transactions between performance and reward rather than forms of interpersonal relationships. As the studies found, this hierarchical model, still evidenced in many organizations, is often rejected by women in positions of power. Rather, women leaders more often see themselves as partners with their followers wherein the leader functions as an inspirational model, mentor and collaborator. Leaders in this transformational model interact with their followers not as 'bosses' but as team leaders and coaches bringing along their mentees to produce results for the organization (Werhane et al., 2007).

Judith Rosener describes this kind of leadership as 'interactive leadership' that entails shared power and information as well as energizing their employees to believe in the value of their contributions and to participate in the organizational decision-making processes. While recognizing that men, too, can and often do engage in interactive leadership, she finds this kind of leadership more prevalent in women executives (Rosener, 1990).

Transformational leaders are usually great communicators with others in their organization, and they do not fear hiring or encouraging managers who could replace them. As Robin Eagly writes:

In this tradition, transformational leadership involves establishing oneself as a role model by gaining followers' trust and confidence. Such leaders delineate organizations' goals, develop plans to achieve those goals, and creatively innovate, even in organizations that are already successful. Transformational leaders mentor and empower their subordinates and encourage them to develop their potential and thus to contribute more effectively to their organization (Eagly, 2007, 2).

Eagly identifies this style of leadership as 'important to leadership, certainly in some contexts and perhaps increasingly in contemporary organizations …' (Eagly, 2007, 2; see also, Rosener, 1990; Eisner, 2013).

James MacGregor Burns, one of the founders along with Bernard Bass of the idea of transformational leadership, creates a third category, 'transforming leadership.' A transforming leader is a person who has a moral vision and seeks to transform her followers to help realize this end. Gandhi, for example, was such a leader (Burns, 1998). We shall present some examples of such leaders in the narratives that follow.

Being a feminine transformational leader is sometimes characterized as 'soft' with those qualities of collaboration and consensus sometimes viewed as less effective than an aggressive, take charge, 'strong' style that is often stereotyped as male. In a male-dominated hierarchical organization it may be challenging for a woman to become a leader without changing her way of leading. But women who adopt such aggressive styles of leadership are often caricatured as too bossy, too aggressive and/or too rigid (Eagly, 2007, 6; see also, Eagly and Johannesen-Schmidt, 2001, 787 and Jamieson, 2010, 37).

> They [women] are expected to be communal because of the expectations inherent in the female gender role, and they are also expected to be agentic because of the expectations inherent in most leader roles. However, because agentic displays of confidence and assertion can appear incompatible with being communal, women are vulnerable to becoming targets of prejudice. Sometimes people view women as lacking the stereotypical directive and assertive qualities of good leaders – that is, as not being tough enough or not taking charge (Eagly, 2007, 4).

Does Gender Make a Difference?

In an article on current leadership styles Susan Eisner reports on leadership styles and gender based on her analysis of interviews published in the *Sunday New York Times* 'Corner Office' series (2013). Eisner found that women focus more on people and relationships than on tasks and results. Women were better at encouraging others and valuing others' worth as individuals. However, many men, too, were good at sharing power and influence, characteristics often attributed to women. None of the women indicated any interest in transactional leadership. Both women and men valued what they called 'authentic leadership' describing such leaders as 'frank, consistent, dependable, self-efficacious, optimistic, resilient [people who] walk the talk' (Eisner, 2013, 30). Referencing Schermerhorn et al. (2010), Eisner notes that leaders orientated toward their followers are often 'engaged in a reciprocal sharing of influence with followers with whom a common vision and goals are then enthusiastically achieved as a result of that partnering' (2013, 30). Both women and men mentioned but did not wholeheartedly adopt a servant-leadership orientation, often understood as leaders who 'are value-driven, seek to affect employees and community positively, listen, earn and keep stakeholder trust, and advance the interest of others before self' (2013, 30). This mild endorsement might have been because the word 'servant' conveys servitude, although the original author of this concept, Robert Greenleaf, was not thinking in those terms. Rather, Greenleaf was trying to emphasize that a leader has obligations, important obligations, to those to whom the leader is responsible, thus it is the leader who is the 'servant' to her managers, employees and workers (Greenleaf, 1977, 2002).

Both men and women were committed to a transformational style of leadership, indicated the importance of mentoring and acknowledged a change in their leadership style. For women the predominant changes in style centered on more effective communications, acquiring a more professional manner and becoming less rigid or bossy. The two latter changes appear to be related to overcoming gender-based perceptions of women leaders and are reflected in Eisner's finding that 'almost one-third of the women commented that gender affected development and career' (2013, 31). In addition to the impact of gender, other attributes that Eisner found are associated with women include a transformational approach to leadership and a concern for enhancing others' self-worth (2013, 34–5).

Eisner concluded that men and women were more alike than previous studies indicate. Both emphasized consensus building, a transformational style, mentorship and a focus on balancing work/life agendas. Both were more concerned with situationally based flexible leadership.

In summary, according to Eisner, as well as other writers including Sweeney (2011) and Greenberg and Sweeney (2005a, 2005b), while men and women work on developing similar leadership styles, it is possible to identify some differences in the manner and motivation for doing so. Both work on being listeners to their constituents; however, 'women leaders are not just listening to form an answer, but really listening, learning, reflecting, then implementing a plan that incorporates the best of everyone's ideas' (Greenberg and Sweeney, 2005b, 35). Likewise, both are concerned with results that, among other qualities, require commitment, determination, and persuasiveness. Women's approach, however, is distinct. Their 'strong people skills ... and willingness to see all sides enhances their persuasive ability' (Greenberg and Sweeney, 2005b, 34). Greenberg and Sweeney believe there is evidence pointing to a new leadership style that women are creating. Citing Jeannette Lichner who claims, 'The female view that we strengthen ourselves by strengthening others is re-defining leadership,' Greenberg and Sweeney note that women leaders 'are assertive, persuasive, empathic, willing to take risks, outgoing, flexible and have a need to get things done' (2005b, 36). They conclude that such 'personality qualities combine to create a leadership profile that, one could easily argue, is much more conducive to today's diverse workplace, where information is shared freely, collaboration is vital and teamwork distinguishes the best companies' (2005b, 36).

Challenges for Women

A recent 2014 study conducted by the Caliper Corporation, a talent management company engaged in leadership development and organizational change, showed that women focus more on people and relationships than on tasks and results. Women were better at encouraging others and valuing their worth as individuals. The

Caliper study also outlined 'five barriers that caused the highest negative impact' for women in organizations. These were:

- Feelings of guilt for not spending enough time with family because of work.
- Family responsibilities interfering with work.
- Resistance from other current leaders.
- Having to outperform male leaders to be considered effective.
- Lack of support in the household when work is demanding (Caliper Research & Development Department, 2014, 5).

Women who see these as barriers are more likely to react negatively to a stereotypical threat. And these women tended to react negatively to transactional forms of leadership even though at work they may be copying a masculine style to avoid being stereotyped as a 'soft' female.

Systems Thinking and Global Leadership

The women we feature in this book are global leaders. While each is physically located in a particular country, their organizations are global organizations. As Nancy Adler once put it, 'Global leaders, unlike domestic leaders, address people worldwide ... A fundamental distinction is that global leadership is neither domestic nor multidomestic: it focuses on cross-cultural interaction' (Adler, 1997, 175; re-quoted in Werhane in Ciulla et al., 2013, volume 3, 16). Moreover, and this is a point that is seldom made in the leadership literature, global leaders must think systemically. A system – whether it is an organization, nation or culture – is a humanly created system. Since human beings are themselves adaptable, all human systems are interactive, dynamic, adaptive and always in a process of change. Together the relationships in such systems are 'the complex interactive dynamic that is productive of adaptive outcomes' (Uhl-Bien et al., 2007, 119). These are often called 'complex adaptive systems.'

The idea that the world is a macro complex adaptive system is not a new one. A good historian will point out that these interrelationships have existed at least since the early explorers and traders. The twenty-first century difference is that the Internet, media, ease of communication and global trading have made these relationships transparent and unavoidable (Friedman, 2007).

A hierarchical transactional leader, proponents of systems thinking argue, does not fit with the complexity of the twenty-first century global macro system where almost every activity is transparent, media discoverable and related in some way or another to every other activity (Friedman, 2007; Uhl-Bien et al., 2007; Collier and Esteban, 2000, the latter two reprinted in Ciulla et al., 2013). This is not merely because of the complex interactions and constant exchanges of data, goods and services. A hierarchical leadership model does not work well in this century because entrepreneurs, managers and executives are themselves constantly adapting to these processes and flux. Thus merely to give or take orders is a detriment to agile, flexible creative thinking that is necessary for success in this environment.

A systems approach to leadership concentrates on the processes of systemic leadership rather than the individual leader. This is because the leader herself is embedded in an organization that itself is part of a global complex system. In this complex global political economy, innovation, adaptability and creativity as well as collaboration are essential components of a successful leader. Werhane and Painter-Morland have not only argued that these characteristics are by and large characteristics of women leaders, but also have gone so far as to conclude that women are or can be more successful global leaders than men because of the demands of operating in such a complex environment (Werhane, 2007; Painter-Morland, 2011). Global leaders, then, according to Adler, should emulate what Gilligan and others have characterized as a feminist style. The women we have included in this book illustrate successful adaptations of this style of leadership.

CONCLUSION

Although leadership styles are steadily morphing into each other, there is still strong evidence that the approaches to leadership of women and men are different. This is often because each socially constructs his or her experiences and concepts of reality in different ways. These socially constructed views of leadership are probably not genetically ingrained, because we see a great deal of evidence that some men as well as a majority of women approach the world as engaged situational leaders who are involved in collaborative enterprises. We also find women leaders who emulate the hierarchical aggressive style often attributed to men. Moreover, what we learned from the Caliper study is that both men and women leaders are becoming more like transformational leaders. In a global world of overlapping complex adaptive systems this form of leadership – transformational and collaborative, with a preoccupation with networking rather than directing – is critical if global change is possible and if enterprises and governments are to survive and thrive in this century.

The ideal of leadership may be the aspiration that 'Good leadership is not male or female; it is simply good leadership' (Beasley, 2005, 92). Our research indicates that we are very far from achieving this ideal despite the stories of the women featured in this book that demonstrate there are women who are extremely good leaders.

PART I

Indian women leaders

Introduction: The Indian context

The complexity of the Indian context places many obstacles in the path of women seeking employment in general, much less those aspiring to senior management and leadership positions. Participation of women in the workforce is among the lowest in the world. Women's 'labour-force participation rate is just 21 percent in urban areas and 36 percent in rural areas' according to the McKinsey Global Institute (MGI) (Dobbs et al., 2015, 7). Not only is there a gender imbalance; there is also gender segregation. Seventy-five percent of 'women are employed in the informal sector and they constitute 23% of the share of total informal sector employment' (Bakshi, 2011, 11). This sector not only includes 'non-regular workers, temporary or part-time workers, piece rate workers, seasonal workers, [and] home-based production workers' (Bakshi, 2011, 12), it also includes self-employed individuals, a category that includes unpaid household workers (Bakshi, 2011, 12).

Indian women's opportunities for education are restricted by social and cultural attitudes and gender bias (Collins and Abichandani, 2016, 13). Even those women who manage to find support and encouragement to pursue educational aspirations that lead to being hired into managerial positions, can find themselves unable to continue in those positions because of social and cultural pressures. This is particularly true for married women, who are impacted by the joint family system, which expects them 'to care for and tend to the in-laws, cook, and clean, in addition to sometimes having a job outside the home' (Collins and Abichandani, 2016, 12). It should be noted that the impact can be uncertain, even after the birth of a child. As Collins and Abichandani note, 'the joint family system can be beneficial for a woman who works because it may provide childcare support from in-laws. It can also be a burden, as Indian women may feel immense pressure to do it all but struggle to find the time, energy, or resources' (Collins and Abichandani, 2016, 14). Even for those who are supported in their desire to work, these social and cultural pressures make it difficult 'to relocate, something that is necessary to climb the corporate ladder' (Rustagi et al., 2013, 19). India has significant numbers of educated women who are underemployed, particularly in urban areas (Collins and Abichandani, 2016). This underemployment is not for lack of aspiration. 'Indian women have been found to be just as ambitious as Indian men' (Wang and McLean, 2016, 103).

However, as the MGI report notes, women are held back by 'deep-rooted attitudes about the role of women in work and society' (Dobbs et al., 2015, iv). Not only, as noted earlier, are they expected to be primary caregivers as well as take on responsibility for household chores, they also 'continue to struggle for basic rights such as minimum wages, equal wages and property rights, in spite of several protective legislations' (Sankaran and Madhav, 2011, 2). Though equality is guaranteed to all in the Indian Constitution, 'the constitutional non-discrimination guarantee, for the most part, is available only in case of abuse by the State,' effectively leaving most women without any protection (Sankaran and Madhav, 2011, 9). This is exacerbated because women's 'access to resources such as land, credit, skill training and education in particular, is relatively poor ...' (Sankaran and Madhav, 2011, 2). In addition to these more universal impediments, women in India face barriers that are unique to their social context.

Among these are concerns for women's safety, particularly in urban areas. The widely reported assaults on women 'such as the 2014 gang rape of a young medical student in New Delhi ... have fueled the public perception that working women in cities are at risk and fortified existing gender stereotypes' (Surie, 2016). A survey conducted after this horrific event highlighted women's concerns and changes in behavior finding 'that 82 percent of women reported leaving work early or before dark to ensure their safety' (Surie, 2016). This is not surprising given that the transportation system in Delhi is ranked by Reuters as the fourth most dangerous for women globally (Reuters, 2014).

Concerns about safety are even greater for women who live alone. Not only does living alone go against societal norms, it can also be difficult to find housing. Most do so for professional or work-related reasons. A study of 500 women living alone in Delhi found that 36 percent 'of respondents cited education and professional training as the reason for living alone, while 33 percent said they lived alone because they were engaged in service-related employment' (Nag, 2016). Many issues confront women who choose to live alone, including:

a lack of safety and security in both the private and public spaces. This ranges from harassment and lewd comments by neighbors, community members, or colleagues; to theft and insecurity at home and in the workplace; to physical violence; and insecurity due to the long work hours or commuting at off-peak hours. In contrast, married women or women living with family often rely on their families for support to confront these challenges ... It is surely a sign of changing times to note that of the total number of women surveyed, 48 percent reported being happy living alone, while 20 percent said they were unhappy (Nag, 2016).

In India, colorism, preferring light skin to dark skin, 'is a customary practice perpetuated by cultural beliefs and values, social institutions (family, educational systems, marriage), and the media' (Sims and Hirudayaraj, 2016, 39). This not only leads to direct discrimination in hiring and promotion, but also can lead to feelings of inferiority. Studies indicate that such 'feelings may cause women to avoid certain positions because they anticipate not being hired based on their complexion or feel unworthy of their positions, particularly if they are aware of the preference of the hiring personnel/organization' (Sims and Hirudayaraj, 2016, 51).

Taken in combination, these factors greatly impede participation in and contribution to the Indian economy, thereby limiting the possibility of women attaining leadership positions in business, government or nonprofit sectors.

CHANGE ON THE HORIZON?

Predictions for the future are mixed. A recent United Nations Development Programme (UNDP) report forecasts that India's working population will be over one billion people by 2050 (2016, 6). It also reported that between 1991 and 2013 the working population rose by 300 million people but the economy created jobs for less than half of them. Given this track record, the report expresses serious concern about the country's ability to generate sufficient numbers of jobs to meet employment demand (UNDP, 2016, 53). This contrasts with other findings that argue India will need 'five million more skilled laborers over the next decade to meet demand' (Shyamsunder and Carter, 2014). 'There is no way to meet that demand without the participation of women' (Collins and Abichandani, 2016, 14). This is echoed by a report of The Asia Foundation that states, 'If India is to become the world's third largest economy in 2030, it can't afford to continue bypassing its over 600 million women from equal opportunity in the workforce' (Surie, 2016).

These latter views have fostered research that, among other things, will provide human resource development specialists with insights into and strategies for bringing educated, skilled women into the workplace and encourage those who leave to have children to return to the workplace.

Some of the suggestions are obvious. These include modifying labor laws so that women are protected in the same way that men are protected and taking up efforts to change social and cultural attitudes about the role of women in both the family and the workplace. In addition, calls for effective mentoring and role models abound (Batra and Reio, 2016, 97). Other suggestions call for organizational changes that will make it more appealing to women to return to work and focus particularly on Indian women returnees, or IWRs. Again, some are more commonplace and 'include offering a bonus for re-entering the workforce or providing benefits, such as flex time and access to career consultants' (Collins and Abichandani, 2016 reported from Kurmanath, 2012). While these strategies have the potential to ease the process of returning to work, they often 'fall flat because they do not address systemic gender oppression' (Collins and Abichandani, 2016, 14).

Perhaps the most interesting of the strategies is providing professional women with a sense of hope. Acknowledging that 'systemic change centers on the evolution of Indian men's attitudes toward women's professional and family roles' (Collins and Abichandani, 2016, 14), Collins and Abichandani argue that nurturing a sense of hope if coupled by some of the changes identified above has the potential to 'provide a strong foundation for change' (Collins and Abichandani, 2016, 14).

They are insistent that the:

> perception that educated and qualified Indian women do not exist should be combated, and issues related to family roles and stereotypes must be addressed in the home and within organizations. We advocate that the education and awareness of men is a crucial aspect of this change, as well as working with IWRs to develop and sustain hope regarding their careers and futures (Collins and Abichandani, 2016, 22).

1. Jeroo Billimoria: Social entrepreneur

Jeroo Billimoria is the founder of nine social ventures, including MelJol, Childline India, Child Helpline International, Aflatoun International and Child and Youth Finance International (CYFI). She is considered one of the world's leading social entrepreneurs. She has been an Ashoka Fellow since 1998 and is a Schwab Fellow of the World Economic Forum. In 2006 she received a Skoll Award for Social Entrepreneurship. She serves on the boards of MelJol, Child Helpline International, Aflatoun International and CYFI. In January 2017 Ms. Billimoria stepped down as Managing Director of CYFI to take some time off for personal growth and development.

This is her story.

Ms. Billimoria was born in Mumbai, India into a family of well-educated professionals who believed in giving back to those who are less fortunate than them. 'My father was an accountant, but socially motivated, always telling us we should give back. My mother was a trained social worker and a professor at the Tata Institute of Social Sciences. My father died when I was 18, but the socially motivated influences of both my parents affected me profoundly early on. At the age of 12,' she recounts, 'I started working with the women who were staff members in our house, enabling them to be self-empowered and to put some of their earnings aside in savings.'

She received a BA in commerce from the University of Mumbai and, with social work strongly ingrained, went on to earn an MA in social work from India's Tata Institute of Social Sciences (TISS). Following that, she attended the New School for Social Research in New York City where she earned an MS in Nonprofit Management. 'During my studies in New York I worked with the Coalition for the Homeless, and that work,' she points out, 'gave me further inspiration and determination to help others.' Having completed her studies she returned to India and traveled the country. 'I started working on an enterprise that failed,' she recalls, 'and then started teaching at Tata Institute of Social Studies.'

It was during that time that she began working on and founded MelJol,[1] which works on furthering the rights of young children, particularly street children. 'One of the initiatives on which we worked involved linking rich children to poor children and to work on peace-building between Hindus and Muslims. What stood out to us the most,' she remarks, 'was just how deeply poverty affected children. So we started focusing on providing social and financial education for these children and instilling the habit of saving at a young age.' This work would later be the foundation for other NGOs she established.

Another aspect of the poverty that affected children, particularly the street children, was the precariousness of many of their lives. 'During our work with street children, I realized that there was a way to connect with them that was already available but not being used – the telephone. In Mumbai and other cities in the 1990s public telephones were ubiquitous on city streets,' she notes, 'so we set up a hotline where street children could call in for help. This gave birth to Childline India. Today, Childline India answers approximately 10 million calls annually.'

Childline[2] was intentionally designed to connect children in need with existing social services and organizations rather than try to replicate those services. The first 24-hour hotline in India, it responds not only to emergency situations but also aids children who are in need of more long-term assistance. While Childline responds to all children, its focus is on the most vulnerable and at risk children. Although that is the primary work of the organization, it also has programs that raise awareness of the plight of children living on the margins of society.

Since 2003 Ms. Billimoria has lived in the Netherlands with her husband, who is Dutch, and her two children. 'It was in the Netherlands that I founded Child Helpline International, Aflatoun and Child and Youth Finance International,' she says. In all three instances, her recognition of the impact of the initiatives she had begun in India was a factor in deciding to take the concepts global.

'Today, in India,' she says, 'many institutions work with children in banking savings schemes. These are part of an Indian government initiative, and NGOs are asked to motivate street children to have savings accounts.' That is what her programs in India were doing. Aflatoun[3] and CYFI[4] are bringing similar initiatives global. Aflatoun works with children in over 100 countries to provide them with social and financial education. One of the hallmarks of its programs is teaching children and youth basic financial skills so that they are able to set goals for themselves and recognize that they have the capacity to change their lives for the better. Similarly, CYFI partners with governments, other NGOs, and financial and educational institutions to help break the cycle of poverty by developing children's entrepreneurial skills, including the financial literacy required for success. It also works with governments and other bodies to advance policies to promote these educational endeavors.

When asked about the challenges she has faced along the way, Ms. Billimoria was clear. 'In India I see that it is difficult to be taken seriously as a young woman, particularly by Indian men of all ages. I remember,' she says, 'I tried to hide my age and dress as an older woman. Surprisingly, when I married and moved to the Netherlands I faced even more problems because I am a woman *and* from India. As an immigrant, I had to build my credibility before I was taken seriously. Moreover, I saw that women in the Netherlands had their own set of struggles. Unlike in India, where there is a strong family support system, the Netherlands has nuclear families, and childcare support options are expensive and limited. This forces many mothers to have to work part-time, or leave work altogether. For me, it helped me to become stronger and create my own solid support network especially with my colleagues. I am fortunate,' she acknowledges, 'to have a very supportive husband who is my rock, and is extremely supportive to all my work and travel, all while being a partner at a major accounting firm.'

In addition to a supportive husband, Ms. Billimoria also acknowledges the influence of mentors and role models. 'I have had many mentors, both men and women. My mother was the most important role model,' she declares. 'A second was Dr. Armaity Desai, formerly Chair of the University Crime Commission and the former Chancellor of the University Grants Commission at the TISS, who was an early supporter of women's rights in India. Although she is retired, I still look to her as a mentor.'

Ms. Billimoria believes the environment is changing for women, particularly in India. 'More Indian women today are working.

When I was a child my mother was the only working woman in my school. There are changing stereotypes about women, too, and these have become positive for young women,' she observes. 'In the Netherlands, too, there is progress for women's rights. When my husband's mother became pregnant she was asked to leave her job. That would not happen today. Moreover, in the Netherlands there is a great deal of respect for what is called "self-made choice." That is, a woman can stay at home or work part-time or work full-time and be respected for that choice.'

Her advice to young women starting to make decisions about career choices is simple. 'Follow your heart and just do what you really want to do. Getting married is a choice, and,' she adds, 'you should avoid the social pressure to do so. But if you decide to marry,' she continues, 'find a supportive spouse where there is equal sharing. Don't give up your career. Do what makes you happy not what you think will make others happy. Argue from a position of strength of your talents and abilities.'

She is adamant that women must believe in themselves. 'As women, we often stop doing that. And sometimes we let rules or worn-out traditions block us and we forget who we are. We all need friends to hold us to our beliefs and commitments and to call out each other to believe in ourselves. We don't all have to be working or have professional careers. The important thing here is for every woman to do what is right for her. No one,' she insists, 'must judge her for that – as long as it is her choice. This is what I believe being a feminist is about.'

LEADERSHIP STYLE

Jeroo Billimoria is a global leader in social entrepreneurial start-ups focusing on children, children's welfare and well-being. With her fearlessness and extraordinary self-confidence, two characteristics critical to women's success as leaders, as well as endless energy and skills in leading these various social programs, she models strong leadership in the nonprofit sector.

NOTES

1. MelJol is an NGO that focuses on developing citizenship skills in school age children, particularly 10 to 15 year olds, by making them aware of their rights and responsibilities. More information about MelJol is available at http://meljol.org/about-us/.
2. Information about the work of Childline India is available at http://www.childlineindia.org.in.
3. Information about Aflatoun International is available at http://www.aflatoun.org.
4. Information about Child and Youth Finance International (CYFI) is available at https://childfinanceinternational.org.

2. Astrid Lobo Gajiwala, Ph.D.: Head, Tata Memorial Hospital Tissue Bank

Astrid Lobo Gajiwala heads the Tata Memorial Hospital Tissue Bank, India's first tissue bank, which she established in 1988. She was India's Project Coordinator for Tissue Banking in an International Atomic Energy Agency sponsored regional tissue bank project, as well as the first woman President of the Asia Pacific Association of Tissue Banking. Dr. Gajiwala is a founding member of Satyashodhak, a Mumbai-based feminist collective that since its inception in 1984 has contributed significantly to the empowerment of women in the Indian Roman Catholic Church. Recipient of two awards for journalism, she contributed to *Catholic Women Speak: Bringing Our Gifts to the Table*, an anthology distributed to the Roman Catholic bishops at the 2015 Synod on the Family, and to *The Strength of Her Witness*, edited by Elizabeth Johnson. She was invited by Voices of Faith as a panelist at a celebration of International Women's Day in the Vatican. Currently, she is on the advisory bodies of a number of international religious reform groups as well as the Jesuit Conference of South Asia (JCSA) and the Jesuit Faculties' Forum for South Asia (JFFSA). Dr. Gajiwala has a Ph.D. in medicine and postgraduate diplomas in tissue banking, bio-ethics and theology.

This is her story.

'In India, we don't divide schooling into high school and middle school; we have 11 classes right through,' Dr. Gajiwala points out as she begins her story. 'In the ninth standard, we have to decide whether we take science or arts. I had a terrific bent for literature and was very good with English and writing and the aptitude test indicated I should be going into the arts. However, I'm the fourth in a family of five children and all my siblings ahead of me had taken science. Instead of the arts, I just followed the family tradition and went into science. I never really had a career in mind. I just drifted into it, I would say. I went on to university, where I did quite well, and graduated with microbiology and chemistry.'

She went on to pursue a masters degree in microbiology though still without a plan. 'I always said my career was kind of like an adventure. I never knew what was going to happen next. I was also working while doing my masters but in the anatomy department. I was learning a lot about histochemistry.[1] This was a completely new subject but I worked in that field while I finished my masters. I got along well with the head of department who was a kind of a mentor at that time,' she recalls. 'He was also a Ph.D. guide and I decided I wanted to study with him; so I switched faculties and joined the medical faculty. I had to go through the exams and do the first and second year subjects, which are the nonclinical academic subjects. That's how I ended up doing my Ph.D. in medicine, though my actual topic was histochemistry, something I never dreamt of studying when I was in school or in college. It just happened.'

'Finding a job was even stranger,' she says. 'I had submitted my thesis and I was waiting for my viva.[2] One day taking the bus home from work I happened to meet a woman I knew from church. We got chatting. She was doing her masters at that time. We were just exchanging notes; I said I was starting to look for a job and didn't know what I was going to do. Actually, I was looking at pharmaceutical companies. Anyway, the conversation ended as we went our separate ways. Maybe half an hour or so after arriving home, I get a call from her. She had mentioned our conversation to her father who was on staff at Tata Memorial Hospital and knew of an opening. I decided I should check it out.'

She learned from the head of the plastic surgery department, who was conducting the interview, that the hospital was interested in starting a tissue bank. 'He had no idea what a tissue bank was and neither did I,' she says. 'He gave me a small spiral-bound manual by a Professor Frank Dexter from the UK and said, "Look, you go through this manual and tomorrow you come back and tell me whether you want to take this on or not." I took the manual home and poured over it the whole night. I decided to give it a shot and went back the next day. He just asked me, "What do you want to do? Do you want to take it on?" I said, "Sure, I'll take it on." That's how I got into tissue banking,' she explains. 'I had no clue what tissue banking was about. I'd never heard of it before. I literally started from scratch. This was in 1986.'

She learned that an International Atomic Energy Agency (IAEA) project had prompted interest in starting a tissue bank. At the time, IAEA was trying to find peaceful purposes for radiation and had initiated a regional project to look at different possibilities, one of which was using radiation to sterilize biological tissues which could then be used for transplants; this would require a way to store tissues that were sterilized with gamma radiation. Because of the department of radiation and oncology, Tata Memorial Hospital was part of the Department of Atomic Energy in India. As a result the sterilization and tissue banking project fell to the hospital.

Dr. Gajiwala faced a number of challenges as she began efforts to establish the tissue bank. 'There was nobody in India who knew anything about them, nobody ahead of me. There was no Internet to use in 1986, so I went to the library and started browsing journals and books to learn anything I could about tissue banks. Then IAEA organized a workshop with Professor Frank Dexter who had written the manual I read to prepare for my job interview. This workshop was in Sri Lanka. I remember,' she states, 'because it was the first time I'd gone abroad. The workshop was very practical and hands-on. I came back and began to work on the tissue bank.'

For the first year she worked alone. 'Finding space was a big problem. I was a bit shocked,' she admits, 'when they showed it to me because it was really a godown[3] in the basement. It had broken windows; there were rats there. My neighbors told me that it flooded during monsoon season. Well, I had no choice. That was it; that was what was given to me.'

The second challenge was organizing the tissue bank. 'Layout is very important in a tissue bank,' Dr. Gajiwala explains. 'Fortunately, I had Professor Dexter's manual with me so was able to plan out the small space, maybe 600 sq ft, and set up our first tissue bank. Within a year I got an assistant. He was not a science student, so I had to train him from scratch, but he was a big help, very good at typing and things like that, so he did a lot of the paperwork. Really, it was a lonely experience,' she reflects. 'Looking back, I often wonder how on earth I had the guts to take it on. I had no idea about processes or anything. I literally learned along the way.'

It took two years of research and planning but by 1988 the tissue bank was ready to open. Though tissue banking had begun in the

1940s and 1950s in Europe and the United States, there were relatively few of them and they operated in an unregulated environment. 'It was very much like a cottage industry,' Dr. Gajiwala recalls. 'Even in the US, the Food and Drug Administration didn't begin regulating tissue banks until about 1993. In India, people were taking what is called surgical residue, like femoral heads, which are removed during hip replacement surgery, putting them in the freezer and then just putting them back into patients. It was totally unregulated. There were no safety norms. Nothing! It was in this environment that I started.'

Once established, there was the challenge of familiarizing people, particularly surgeons, with the concept of a tissue bank. 'Surgeons were not used to these tissues, to banked tissues,' she points out, 'so I had to create a market. To create a market, you have to convince people to use it, that it's good and it's safe. Again, it was very difficult. It took me years before I could get some of our own Tata Hospital doctors, surgeons, to say yes, they're willing to try using the tissues. Of course, once they did and it worked there was no looking back.'

'The third difficulty that I faced was that we were a cancer hospital. There are two types of tissue donors,' she explains. 'You can have deceased donors who, if they pass all the screening requirements, are potential donors for tissues. Tata is a cancer hospital and cancer patients cannot be donors; none of the deaths at Tata Hospital can be converted into donors. I had to look elsewhere. The second place that you can get donor tissue,' she continues, 'is from surgical or medical residue. For instance, femoral heads or tibia slices, which are removed for medical reasons and would normally be thrown out, can be given to a tissue bank. Once sterilized, a femoral head can be crushed into chips or blocks used for packing or various forms of reconstruction. I need to be connected to general hospitals in order to get such donated tissue.'

The same difficulty exists in securing donations of amnion, a membrane of the amniotic sac usually discharged when a baby is delivered. According to Dr. Gajiwala, 'the amnion offers an excellent biological dressing which we produce in our bank. Here, I have to be connected to a maternity hospital. Building all of these networks took a lot of time and effort. It also took time to build awareness among user surgeons and to build their confidence in the tissue so they could see that they could use these grafts safely and efficiently. Once we did that,' she states, 'I felt the need to assess what we were doing.'

Her involvement with the IAEA project proved to be helpful in that endeavor. She had been involved in training programs for those interested in starting tissue banks as well as a member of the committee that established standards for tissue banks, which she used to organize the tissue bank at Tata. 'Since there were no regulators, I decided to have an external audit. I used the ISO quality management system.[4] It was not exclusively for tissue banks,' she acknowledges, 'and it didn't question the standards or protocols, but required that you demonstrate that you were following them, which for me was good enough. We did this in 2004 and were India's first ISO compliant tissue bank. We had a lot of firsts,' she points out, 'including, after much persistence, the first tissue bank to be registered in India.'

Eventually, demand started increasing, in part because two of the surgeons at the hospital began to present papers at national and international orthopedic conferences detailing their success in using grafts from the tissue bank. 'Of course,' Dr. Gajiwala admits, 'with the demand increasing we had to step up with the donations and we had to step up with the facilities and infrastructure, knowing space was at a premium. Tata Hospital is a fantastic cancer hospital, but the focus is cancer. The tissue bank is not directly related to cancer; it's totally service oriented. It took time and patience, but I must say that Tata Hospital has been a great place to work. I understand the constraints and recognize we're not a priority department, but at the same time there was a lot of support. In 2000, we got the extra space and expanded a bit and I got more staff in. Today, we're ten people working in the tissue banks where initially I was just one. In 2015, though we didn't get more space, we were able to renovate the whole space; we needed that badly. As we grew,' she explains, 'we didn't revamp, so we didn't grow in a very organized manner. Now it looks quite good, if I may say so myself. Small as it is, it's very compact but as someone said who came to see it, "I can't believe you can do that good work in this small space." It functions well now so we are on maintenance mode and ready for the next stage, wherever research takes us.'

Reflecting on her journey, Dr. Gajiwala comments, 'When somebody asks me to do something, I just say yes. I feel that I'll find the means, and I'll find the resources to be able to handle it. The second thing that I find about myself is whenever I take on a job I give it my best. It doesn't matter whether it's a small job or a big one. I just put in all the effort that I can. I have this thing – maybe it comes from my mother who was a bit of a perfectionist – whatever job I do, I need to shine. With the tissue bank I didn't think that far ahead, but at every stage, whatever I did, I gave it my best. Things fell into place after that. Maybe if I had thought about the whole thing, I would have asked, "How am I ever going to do that?" But I didn't, I just thought, "OK, this needs to be done right now!" and I just did it.'

She brought this same attitude to her involvement in the Asia Pacific Association of Surgical Tissue Banking (APASTB). 'A lot of the members are surgeons,' she says, 'mostly orthopedic surgeons; they were the ones hosting the conferences which are held every two years. In fact, once there was a woman who was more active, but the male surgeon was named the host and so was president of APASTB for that term. I thought to myself, let me see if I can manage to host, so I agreed to host the conference at Tata Memorial Hospital. To my bad luck, IAEA had stopped funding this conference. In the past IAEA would have its meeting of the regional national coordinators – I was the coordinator for India – timed in such a way that the APASTB conference would follow. So, everything including our travel was funded by the IAEA.'

She did not let the change in circumstances deter her. 'The tissue bank community is a very small community, but as I said, I just get into things and so I did. I realized that when you have something like this, you shouldn't go it alone. You need to get people involved,' she declares. 'I got as many collaborators as I could from the different departments at Tata Hospital. People in radiation therapy use our amnion for skin reactions that happen after radiation, so I got the head of the radiation department involved. I got someone from the Bhabha Atomic Research Centre. I got immunologists and some of our oncologists involved and orthopedic surgeons, too. They were all part of my organizing committee. I must say it was really amazing, and they all brought in funds. We had no issues with funding at all,' she emphasizes.

Overcoming funding was not, however, the most significant thing about her term as president and the conference she hosted. 'It was also the first conference the Asia-Pacific tissue bank community had which was attended by people from so many different faculties,' she notes. 'We had a number of simultaneous workshops on topics such as stem cells, orthopedic and plastic surgery, and dental and oral work. Each of the sessions attracted its own specialists. In the end, we had a really good group and had the largest number of people attending. When I look back, it was a great experience and a tremendous success. I was happy to be the first woman president of the Asia Pacific Association of Surgical Tissue Banking,' she admits. 'I think that broke a glass ceiling because it was after 19 years of the association's existence.'

Her leadership skills and persistent spirit led to another first – regulation of the tissue bank industry in India. 'I was very worried about the lack of regulation,' Dr. Gajiwala recalls. 'The Transplantation of Human Organs Act was set in 1994. It was geared mainly for organs: kidney, liver and organs like that. Basically, it was to prevent commercialization of organs. Unfortunately, the definition of organs was such that it was very ambiguous and could also have included the tissues. We started advocating for a change in that law. I was quite instrumental because I was the only one who knew anything about tissues. A lot of changes also needed to be made as regards organs. Corneas were very well looked after by the eye banks, which are very well developed in India, so they had everything in place. But for the remaining tissues like skin and bone there was nobody, so I was pushing for that. Eventually, the government called me as an expert for the tissue aspect. We had a number of meetings with people from various areas. Finally, in 2011, the law was amended. It actually takes tissues into account and now all tissue banks have to be officially registered. This is a great thing,' she emphasizes. 'Tissue banks get inspected by the director of health services and have to have certain basic standards. I'm very happy and proud to be associated with this, which is so important for the country.'

Asked about barriers she faced, Dr. Gajiwala was clear that she did not face any barriers because she was a woman. She did acknowledge, however, that when she first joined Tata in 1986 there was not much gender balance, particularly at senior levels. 'I think much changed after we got a woman as director from 1995 to 2008. She was quite conscious of the whole gender issue. She gave many women charge of their departments and there were also many new women recruits who continue in service. There's been no looking back since,' she declares. 'I draw attention to this to make the point that gender sensitive directors, whether female or male, can have far reaching consequences. At present, 63 percent of the departments are headed by women, which is very good. By and large, I would say that we don't have a gender issue in the hospital and I have seen women are very assertive and confident.'

Dr. Gajiwala has clear advice for younger women aspiring to be successful and move into leadership positions. 'I would say, believe in yourself. That's the most important first step. By the way,' she points out, 'I have two daughters in their twenties who are more feminist than I am. I tell them the same. The second thing I would say is to be passionate about what you do. It's only if you're passionate about what you do that you'll be able to give it your all. When you do that, then you do an excellent job and everything automatically falls into place.'

'While you need to keep the big picture in mind,' she concedes, 'you need to prioritize, take the jobs as they come, live one day at a time and give it your best shot. I think it's important to be seen as reliable and dependable. Over the years, I've been able to build up that kind of reputation. People feel that if they come to me with a job, it will be well done. I think it's important in life; you should have that kind of credibility. Another thing, I would advise is to say yes to every opening that you get. Don't worry about how qualified you are or whether you have the resources; just jump in. You'll find yourself and find your way. This is important,' she argues, 'because I think you always need to push yourself out of your comfort zone. It's only then that you grow and only then that you're able to achieve great things, because you start searching and when you search you find. I know that sounds very Biblical, but the point is you will find doors opening up, you will meet people, you will find references, whatever.'

'The other thing I've learned is that when you say yes to opportunities you grow and learn a lot. I don't mean only opportunities in your field. I have,' she continues, 'what might be considered a parallel career in the church. I've often thought a lot of the skills I've learned in the church, I've been able to use in my job. From a very young age – way before I got married – I've been involved in women's groups and other parish groups, being secretary, reporting at meetings and so forth. All of this honed my skills in terms of listening, in terms of synthesizing, in terms of being able to write reports, in terms of public speaking. All of this became part of my personality. It's similar to the speech and drama examinations my mother made my sister and I do when we were in school,' she notes. 'An examiner came from London every year to conduct the speech and drama exams. Both my sister and I excelled in them. It helps because you're able to speak when you're in a group, when you're on an international stage. It really, really helps. I think these are some of the things that come from outside my tissue banking career that have helped me and are why I think it's important to say yes. Of course, it should be something that interests you. Obviously, I'm not talking about things that don't interest you, but if it's something that interests you, then I think you should go for it and then work on it.'

Her final piece of advice has to do with boundaries. 'I think an important aspect of succeeding is not to recognize boundaries,' Dr. Gajiwala insists. 'My entire adult life has been lived across boundaries with a marriage that is inter-religious and inter-cultural. Fighting to get my voice heard from the margins of the church in a way prepared me for the struggle to get my tissue bank on the map decades before its time, and in the process, help to shape and develop the field of tissue banking in India.'

LEADERSHIP STYLE

Dr. Astrid Lobo Gajiwala displays a number of qualities as a female leader. The first is that she is well educated; that background gave her the courage to accept the assignment of the founder of the first tissue bank in India, although she did not know at that time what a tissue bank was. This fearlessness and determination not to fail exemplify characteristics of women leaders who succeed despite the odds, in this case the lack of knowledge about tissue banks.

She is in an inter-religious marriage to a Hindu while maintaining her faith, which in turn has led to various leadership positions in the Roman Catholic Church. She also has two daughters. Dr. Gajiwala is an exemplary model of a woman who has not forsaken her strong religious beliefs or her roles as wife and mother while pursuing a very successful professional career.

NOTES

1. Histochemistry is the process of working with cells and/or tissues to determine the chemical components between and within cells.
2. Viva is the term used for oral examinations or oral defense of a thesis or dissertation.
3. Godown is a term for warehouse or storage space; commonly used in Asia.
4. ISO is the acronym for the International Organization for Standardization, an independent NGO based in Geneva, Switzerland that develops and publishes international standards for a wide range of industries and services. More information is available at http://www.iso.org/iso/home.htm.

3. Corinne Kumar: International Coordinator and Founder, World Courts of Women

Corinne Kumar has dedicated her life to working for human rights and advocating alternate models of development. She founded the World Courts of Women in 1992 and continues as the coordinator. For more than 20 years she served as Secretary General of El Taller, an international NGO committed to working with civil society organizations to address issues of poverty, underdevelopment and women's rights. Ms. Kumar was a founding member of the Centre for Informal Development Studies, of the Asian Women's Human Rights Council and of Vimochana, an NGO in Bangalore, India concerned with domestic violence, dowry-related deaths and workplace sexual harassment. Editor of *Asking, We Walk: The South as a New Political Imaginary*, a four-volume set of essays, she has also published numerous journal articles. She is considered to be a poet by many who know her.

This is her story.

As a young woman, Corinne Kumar intended to follow in her father's footsteps as an officer in the Indian diplomatic corps. She was working on a doctoral degree and preparing for the foreign service examinations when a chance meeting disrupted her plans. Taking a tea break from her studies, she shared a table with an older gentleman. After exchanging pleasantries, he asked about her work.

'I told him all of the things I was studying and researching,' she recounts. 'I was kind of full of myself at the time. I was used to everyone saying, "she's so young and she's doing all of this." This man just laughed and said, "Look at you, every bit a city girl. What do you know about the rural areas? What do you know about development? What do you know about the poor? You'll probably write a book, and it will end up on some library shelf." I was crying inside, thinking what is with this man, he doesn't understand what I am saying. But he continued, "Something about you is different." He then took out a piece of paper, wrote down an address, and suggested I visit him.'

The man, she learned, was Vincente Frère, a Spanish Jesuit priest. He had been organizing farmers and landless laborers in the state of Maharashtra. Seen as a threat, he was told by the state government he could no longer work in Maharashtra. Ironically, Ms. Kumar relates, 'the chief minister of Andhra Pradesh invited him to work in Rayalaseemsa one of the state's poorest districts.' Against her mother's better judgment, Ms. Kumar decided to accept the invitation to visit him there. 'I told my mother I was going, that it was only for two days, just the weekend, and I'd be back in time for my exams. It was the beginning of the first part of my story.'

As it turned out, the two-day weekend visit turned into a two-year stay. 'I remember the first day,' she reflects. 'I saw him just pick up this child with leprosy. He just held the child, like Mother Teresa in some ways. But there he was being so natural and continuing talking to everybody. He had what I would call a kind of unconditional love for everybody. This is probably the central value of our lives. If we learn that and if we give that, it's the biggest secret of this life,' she insists.

Those two years were 'years of unlearning,' she declares. 'I had to unlearn all of the things I'd been taught by those in positions of power and privilege. They teach you their ways so you can become part of the power and privilege system.' Living in the village was different. 'I started to walk the alternative, walk with people on the margins,' she explains. 'Most of all I learned the real meaning of compassion from Vincente Frère. We all feel sad, we feel empathetic even, but compassion is something much deeper. You almost become the other.'

During those years she began reading Karl Marx's *Das Kapital*; there was a growing Marxist movement in India at the time but it didn't fully appeal to her. 'I knew from the deepest part of me,' she says quietly, 'that I could never choose any way that was violent. There was a non-violent way that drew me, that the people taught me,' she says. 'They taught me to put my ears to the ground, so to speak, to listen in a different way,' she recalls.

When she returned home she started the Centre of Informal Education and Development Studies (CIEDS), a collective based in Bangalore which is still going strong more than 40 years later. It was, and continues to be, a place where serious consideration is given to alternative models of development. 'In the 1970s when we began the model was only an economic development model that dispossessed the majority of people with the rich in India getting richer and the poor poorer,' Ms. Kumar asserts. 'That economic development model desacralized nature, dispossessed people and denigrated women; it was not the answer.'

She recognized that others were also looking for alternatives, but found people from the different movements were not speaking with one another. That recognition was the catalyst. 'I decided we needed a place where we on the left could speak with each other.' Another critical aspect was ensuring a pluralistic way of looking at life. 'In India,' Ms. Kumar points out, 'you cannot be dogmatic; there is too much diversity. So, pluralism became part of the center, where all kinds of people from all sorts of religions or none were engaged in justice issues. The common ground was justice and a concern for human rights. We were in this place that was somewhere in between the universal human rights discourse of the West and the culturally specific discourse that rejects the universal discourse.'

For Ms. Kumar, the fruits of universal discourse must be infused with cultural specificity. 'We can choose *a* central mountain or many central mountains. We can talk of *a* story or of many stories. It is in the many stories that we find the seeds of another dialogue, of other politics. It is a way in which we find multiple layers of knowledge,' she insists. 'I think this is true whether you look at the development sector, rights discourse or, as we say today, the rights of Mother Nature.' For her, this pluralistic perspective is directly related to dialogue with others. 'For example,' she adds, 'we learn from encounters with indigenous people who don't see nature only as resource. They help us look at different ways to articulate alternative visions that challenge the system and some standard discourses.'

As a result of her work, she was often invited to speak on issues of political thought and human rights. On one occasion she found herself on a panel with Ivan Illich,[1] a controversial critic of institutions, and two others. 'I was passionately presenting my

Marxist analysis when suddenly I got a little note. It was from Ivan Illich; it said, "We need to take a walk." I have never forgotten that little note. After we had finished, we went for a walk, and he tore me up – tore up my paper, tore up everything on that walk. "Why have you filled your head with this garbage?" he asked and then said, "Somewhere, in all that rubble, I saw a spark but it is so tiny you will have to do an archaeological kind of exercise to find that spark. But I think you are capable of doing that, you will find that spark." I immediately thought of Fr. Vincente and realized this was another turning point for me.'

The result for Ms. Kumar was a move away from Marxism. 'I started to read more Gandhi, more about alternative thinkers including feminists. Slowly I began to be very Third World, very South[2] in my thinking and I still am,' she declares. Meanwhile, she was working with the Asian Women's Human Rights Council. It was a time when violence against women was escalating but there was little success at redress. Rights activists wondered why, despite the number of cases filed for dowry burning in India, none had been won. The justice system was not working for these women. Ms. Kumar and others began questioning the operative mental models, or frames as she calls them.

'I started thinking about it,' she recalls, 'and realized there is no justice for women simply because the frames we are using are gender blind. They are patriarchal; women are not included in those frames. We needed to find a way outside those frames to provide an alternative justice mechanism for the women.' The result was the World Courts of Women. 'It is not a sanctioned legal court,' Ms. Kumar states, 'but it provides a respectful venue for the women to speak, to tell the truth of their experience. There are tears. They speak of their trauma, of the brutality they have experienced. They are believed. It is, they tell me, the beginning of their healing.'

In addition to the women who testify and their many supporters, the structure of the World Courts of Women includes a panel of experts. These experts come from a wide variety of disciplines. They might be professors, activists, social workers, attorneys, theologians, poets or artists. They are charged to listen to the testimony, compile and assess it and create a report of their findings. The reports are then presented to international organizations concerned about women's development and empowerment.

The first court, held in Lahore, Pakistan in 1992, focused on domestic violence, dowry burning, acid throwing, honor crimes and rape.

Soon after the first court and recently widowed, Ms. Kumar moved to Tunisia to take up the position of Secretary General of El Taller International. Established in April 1992 with Nelson Mandela a founding member and President of the Board of Directors, the NGO and its staff were granted diplomatic status by the government of Tunisia. Created to bring together various individuals and groups working for non-violent social transformation, under Ms. Kumar's direction El Taller fostered dialogue on alternative responses to the dominant discourse on human rights, development and security at regional and global levels. Much of this was done by partnering with other NGOs to develop programs on thematic issues; this offered a way to bring the voices of those on the margins into the center as well as provide alternatives to overcome negative aspects of globalization particularly as they impact human rights and women's rights. The World Courts of Women was among the programs. One that was particularly memorable for Ms. Kumar was the 2001 court, a three-day event held in Cape Town, South Africa. Archbishop Desmond Tutu was among those who addressed the participants and listened to the testimony of women who suffered various forms of violence.

The work at El Taller was challenging on many levels. 'We made El Taller a place for poets and writers and intellectuals. We had round tables, poetry evenings and storytelling circles. There were all kinds of political stories about the region. Then in 2005 Tunisia hosted a world summit on the information society and the digital divide. Ben Ali, who was president, spoke about a digital divide that would accentuate the poverty divide in the world. I picked that one sentence,' she recounts, 'and I wrote a proposal to start a communication technology center. It was very creative. We started to train batches of young people in communication technology. We went to the poor neighborhoods and sought out children who had no schools. We trained them in Internet media, which they picked up just like that,' she says snapping her finger. 'It was fascinating to work in Tunisia, but it became more difficult even with diplomatic status. It had become a dictatorship under Ben Ali. Our calls were being monitored. I was being followed around. I had always managed to ease the concerns of the government when they called me in to ask about our work,' she recounts, 'but there came a day when it seemed my answers weren't accepted.' After almost 20 years in Tunisia and under constant pressure from the Tunisian government, she knew it was time to leave. 'I decided it was time to come home to India. I was not able to stay longer,' she acknowledges. 'I felt I needed to spend the evening of my life in India, to finish the work I began at home.'

Much of her life's work is represented in her writings and books, particularly her four-volume anthology *Asking, We Walk: The South as a New Political Imaginary*. 'In this work I meet so many wonderful people who come into my life and we become such good friends. I got up one morning and I decided to ask these friends of mine to write their best critical cutting-edge essay about a turning point in their lives and a turning point in the discourse. The essays tried to make the South not South as Third World only, but South as alternative knowledge, subjugated peoples, silenced voices,' she explains. 'I was looking at the South in these ways as movements of people, and I began looking at the South as powerless. I wanted us to look at that and critique. But I also wanted us to look at the darker side of modernity: slavery, colonialism and globalization. It is a kind of trajectory. I also wanted an analysis of "isms," like Gandhism,[3] Zapatismo[4] and Ujamaa[5] in Tanzania.'

The first volume critiques the status quo and provides alternative versions of human development. The second volume examines the manner in which those alternatives work, while the third volume presents a de-colonial discourse that considers modernity. The fourth volume looks at lived alternatives and describes the work and struggles of those committed to such change and transformation.

'All through the books, I wanted rational academic essays but I also wanted stories. I looked for the poets, for the resistance movements. These are all sprinkled right through. The books are put together with some of the best thinkers. I'm just the weaver,' she insists, 'and have written an essay here and there to give the series a frame. I always look for those who are not walking the straight line but who are getting lost in the forest. There is much to learn working with them, listening to them.' She mentions Julia, who attended one of the Courts of Women. 'As she passed me,' Ms. Kumar recounts, 'she squeezed a little note into my hand and said to read it later. In the note she writes only about love. A person who doesn't eat, who lives on the street, she only wrote about love. If we were only to say that to each other all the time. We need that kind of voice of wisdom,' she softly insists. 'Working with so many people, listening to so many stories, I realize how little I know and how little I can do by myself. I could never work without this collective that works in a way that is modest, that is sincere, that is humble in a way. These alternative voices come from everywhere in the world, from people who resist and rebel and dare to dream. That's who I work with, the dreamers.'

Settled once again in Bangalore, her hometown, she continues her work and has organized another session of the World Courts of Women.[6] She continues to join others working for peace, justice and an end to violence against women and to challenge the young dreamers with whom she works as Vincente Frère and Ivan Illich once challenged her, albeit in a gentler way.

LEADERSHIP STYLE

Corinne Kumar is a spiritual leader. Her ideas inspire others to work for justice for the poor and brutalized, particularly women in emerging economies. She is a modern-day Gandhi whose ideas led the revolution in India. Her leadership reminds us of the importance of values-based ideas in leadership. More importantly, she brings voices from the South, from emerging economies and from the neglected poor and enslaved to our consciousness, and these are the voices global leaders must pay attention to if they are to be successful in this century.

NOTES

1. Ivan Illich was a controversial critic of institutions and modern technological developments arguing that they inhibited human freedom and self-sufficiency. More details on his life are available at http://www.telegraph.co.uk/news/obituaries/1415202/Ivan-Illich.html.
2. 'South' or 'Global South' refers to the world's developing countries most of which are in the southern hemisphere.
3. Gandhism refers to the thoughts and ideas of Mohandas Karamchand Gandhi, a leader in India's independence movement who was particularly known for his support of non-violent civil disobedience.
4. Zapatismo refers to a grassroots movement that focuses on the rights of indigenous peoples, works for social reforms and fights against all forms of

oppression – cultural, economic and spiritual. More information is available at http://www.oxfordreference.com/view/10.1093/oi/authority.20110803133357216.
5. *Ujamaa* is Swahili for 'kinship' or 'familyhood' and refers to the village collectives that were part of the socialist experiment of Julius Nyerere, a leader in Tanzania's independence movement and the country's first president. More information is available at http://www.encyclopedia.com/people/social-sciences-and-law/sociology-biographies/julius-nyerere.
6. A report on the court by Dr. Rebecca Johnson, FRSA, who is on the panel of experts that hears testimony is available at https://www.opendemocracy.net/5050/rebecca-johnson/courts-of-women-resisting-violence-and-war.

4. Sharma Sujata, Ph.D.: Director, Tapan Rehabilitation Society

Dr. Sharma Sujata is the founder and Director of the Tapan Rehabilitation Society. Located in Karnal, India, it is a nonprofit organization serving special needs children through a range of services and programs. Prior to that she had a short tenure as senior consultant in the psychiatry department of Metro Group Hospitals in New Delhi and was a project officer with UNICEF. Dr. Sujata holds a doctoral degree in psychology and a postgraduate degree in guidance and counseling.

This is her story.

Dr. Sujata did not intend her life's work to focus on special needs children and young adults. 'I had never thought of entering this line of occupation after attaining my degree,' she says. 'I was just following whatever came my way. I was never a career woman; I am very shy and introverted. But now after much enlightenment I can say we don't choose our occupations but it's vice versa. It chooses us.'

By the time she finished her studies she wanted to become a counselor. 'I started my career as a project officer in UNICEF for three years,' she says. 'I also served patients with anxiety, trauma, phobias and many distresses during a short tenure with the Metro Group Hospitals.' She had no plans to establish or lead anything, but as she put it, 'a group of differently disabled children approached me for guidance and I felt that need to extend my services at that time.'

That was the beginning of Tapan Rehabilitation Society, what she calls, 'my brain child.' Initially it served 25 children with a range of needs providing services such as speech therapy and vocational training. Today it has grown to include Viklang Shishu Prashikshan Kendra, a residential institution for children and young adults ranging in age from 3 to 30 years old. Doctors, social workers and educators have joined Dr. Sujata to work together with students, educating them and teaching them daily living skills that will help them better integrate into the day-to-day life of their communities. A range of opportunities each geared to students' various abilities is available including prevocational and vocational training.[1]

While the work is rewarding, it has not always been easy. 'The journey was very tough,' Dr. Sujata says. 'It was not easy to make people aware of the therapies for persons with special needs.' Part of her challenge has been raising awareness of possibilities and options beyond simply providing care. In addition, as she notes, 'Parents don't want to spend for their disabled children and people in India do charity only for religious institutions, orphanages and so on. So, finances remain a major concern for us.' Despite this, she has managed to continue the work for almost a quarter of a century.

Her attitude and leadership style have, no doubt, contributed to her success. 'I am a self-motivated woman. I have always set my own targets and achieved them,' she says. She acknowledges that 'in India women face pressures maintaining a balance between home and careers. Even at work it is sometimes hard to face your male subordinates. Over the years this scenario has changed but only in certain areas.' She insists that if women are to succeed and fulfill their dreams they need 'to respect themselves and have confidence in their abilities to achieve their goals.' They also need a support system and mentors.

Giving credit to her family, she says they 'supported my dreams though sometimes hesitantly; my parents were instrumental to my success.' The middle child of three daughters, she comes from a highly educated family. 'My father has a doctorate in Upanishads and History. He retired as class I officer in the Education Department. He is a poet and has written three books. My mother is a highly intellectual homemaker with high expectations for her daughters. My father brought us up as sons, giving education to all three of us.' Her elder sister has a doctorate in history and has served with the United Nations in several different countries. Her younger sister has an M.Phil. in English, and she and her husband live in Indonesia where she teaches at one of the international schools.

Dr. Sujata had support and encouragement from others as well. She notes that many 'have played a significant role in my journey. I have noticed whenever there was a barrier along the way these people have helped to remove it. This has happened many times in a long journey of 25 years. Men and women both have helped and their help has opened a new dimension in my journey.' In referring to these mentors she mentions in particular her spiritual guru while acknowledging that 'some people also were negative mentor-gurus in life.' In the end, however, she says all of them together 'made me what I am today.'

She herself is a mentor. 'I always keep in mind the struggle I have faced,' she says and 'help other souls like me in several ways to achieve their dreams. I have been and I am a role model for many women.' She continues, 'I feel privileged when women say that they want to become like me; only then do I explain my journey of struggle and how I turned negative circumstances into positive ones.' She is emphatic, 'I advise them, "Always stick to your values and never sacrifice your dreams for short term material gains." I think every woman should help other women, to empower them in all spheres of life because we never know what their particular battles are. Above all, I want every woman to love and have respect for what she is. After all she is the creator who is now a provider as well.' She is convinced, 'that if society as a whole would give support by way of family or government or people in positions of power, women can outgrow their traditional roles and rule the planet in a more balanced way.'

Asked what motivates her to continue her work after all these years, she responds without hesitation. 'My faith in God remained my only strength. I gave 100 percent in every situation but I remained unattached. I have a strong belief that God has sent me for a cause and he is there to assist me to accomplish it.'

LEADERSHIP STYLE

Sharma Sujata is a self-motivated servant leader. She sees herself as doing God's work by helping the mentally disabled as her mission, and she has served that community for over 20 years. She is also a model of values-based leadership, pursuing her goals by creating and sustaining Tapan with perseverance and determination. She is thus able to empower other women by her example. The motto for Tapan is, 'Every individual is unique and can contribute to the society in a meaningful way, if given right input at right time.' That motto, written by Dr. Sujata, expresses her philosophy and lifelong project.

NOTE

1. Information on Tapan Rehabilitation Society and the residential institution is available from: Dutt (2000), Arora (2013) and http://tapanrehab.org.

PART II

Japanese women leaders

Introduction: The Japanese context

Women in Japan seeking to be successful leaders work in an environment that places many obstacles in their path. One is the practice of lifetime employment, long a hallmark of the Japanese way of doing business. Though there has been a movement away from this practice, much support for it still exists (Nemoto, 2013, 154). Those fortunate enough to be hired into positions that promise lifetime employment are known as 'regular' workers and, traditionally, have been men. Governmental social policies, such as tax deductions and other benefits, provide disincentives for women to work full-time and foster a 'male breadwinner model of work and family' (Nemoto, 2013, 154). This has led to significant numbers of women being engaged in part-time, 'non-regular' work.

Another obstacle is the two-track hiring system in corporate Japan whereby some, again predominantly men, are hired straight out of university for career track jobs that eventually lead to managerial positions, including senior leadership positions. Others are hired in non-career or area-career tracks, neither of which includes 'the same benefits and promotion opportunities as career-track workers' (Nemoto, 2013, 155). This has resulted in gender-based vertical segregation with a 'concentration [of working women] in clerical and low-level management positions' (Nemoto, 2013, 154). In 2014, Catalyst reported that women accounted for only 5.6 percent of those employed in career track jobs. The report also noted that 65 percent of Japanese women in career track jobs leave within ten years. Of those who remain for ten years, only 35.5 percent have moved into managerial positions compared to 55.4 percent of their male colleagues (Catalyst, 2014).

Women fortunate enough to be hired into regular, career-track positions face obstacles stemming from organizational culture and expectations of career track employees exemplified by the Japanese *sarariiman*, or salarymen, the term used for these employees. Loyalty to the company is of utmost importance and often trumps loyalty to family. The working week includes Saturdays and the already long workday, with its unavoidable unpaid overtime, is extended on a regular basis by socializing with business colleagues, which is de rigueur for salarymen. More often than not this socialization takes place in hostess clubs or *izakayas*, local tavern or pub-like establishments that serve food; often women co-workers are not included which can result in women being excluded from important networking and mentoring opportunities.

Job rotation is a standard practice in Japanese companies; given the broad perspective of a company's business that results from working in various departments and divisions, it is an integral aspect of moving into managerial positions and advancing a career. Job rotation usually results in relocation domestically and on occasion internationally. In some instances, such moves are *tanshin funin*, or solo transfers, with family not accompanying the employee. Since these transfers are a normal part of the career path, women, particularly those with responsibilities for children or elderly relatives, are at a disadvantage (Roberts, 2011, 585–6).

Women with children face additional challenges in light of societal perspectives that view mothers as the primary caregivers for children. This is coupled with the fact that it is the mother who is ordinarily the parent responsible for children's successful education. Given the importance in Japanese society of attaining a quality education, it is not surprising that 60 percent of women stop working after the birth of their first child (Catalyst, 2014).

CHANGE ON THE HORIZON?

There are signs of change on the horizon, though expectations are that this change will continue to be slow in coming. Some argue changes in demographics make change inevitable. The population is aging, placing greater demands on adult children to care for parents. This is coupled with one of the lowest fertility rates in the world and a declining population. As the World Economic Forum notes, 'the most important determinant of a country's competitiveness is its human talent' (Catalyst, 2014). Government policies appear to recognize this, with Prime Minister Shinzo Abe taking the lead in what is dubbed Abe's Womenomics, with a call to increase the number of women participating in the workforce. In addition, moves have been made to encourage adoption of more flexible hours, provision of better childcare and senior-care, and implementation of other programs that foster better work-life balance for women. To that end, in a 2013 speech to the UN General Assembly Abe announced $3 billion had been designated for use in addressing these issues (UN News Centre, 2013). Arguably, the hallmark of Abe's Womenomics is his goal for women to hold 30 percent of managerial positions in Japan by 2020 (Davidson, 2014).

Increasing the number of women in the workforce has the potential to impact economic growth significantly. If women's workforce participation rates were the same as men's workforce participation rates, it is estimated that Japan's GDP would increase by 13 percent to 15 percent (World Economic Forum, 2014; Auslin, 2015; Iinuma and Black, 2014). Corporate performance is also a consideration. 'Global research has shown that companies in the top quartile of female participation in top management outperform peers with no female participation by fully 56 percent in terms of earnings before interest and taxes' (World Economic Forum, 2014). Evidence indicates that Japanese companies can expect the same improved performance (World Economic Forum, 2014).

Despite the strong economic case made for fuller participation of women in the workplace, Abe's 2020 targets have 'been dramatically scaled back, with officials conceding that the ambition "was not shared by society as a whole"' (Lewis, 2016, 3). Modifications and adjustments in various governmental policies and corporate practices are not sufficient to change the long-standing male-dominated workplace culture. It is interesting to note that many of those who follow the slow progress women have made in Japan call for more role models for today's Japanese women hoping to be among Abe's 30 percent (World Economic Forum, 2014; Catalyst, 2014; Iinuma and Black, 2014).

5. Hisa Anan: Independent Director, Megmilk Snow Brand Co., Ltd.

Ms. Anan has been an outside independent director of Megmilk Snow Brand Co., Ltd. since her appointment in June 2015. She also serves as a director of the Association to Create a Society with Consumer Citizenship. From 2012 to 2015 she served as Secretary General of the Consumer Affairs Agency established by the government in 2009. Prior to that Ms. Anan, who has had an active career in consumer rights, was Secretary General of Shodanren, the National Liaison Committee of Consumer Organizations; she succeeded Ms. Nobuko Hiwasa (see Chapter 6) in this position.

This is her story.

Following her university education, Ms. Anan taught high school part time. After the birth of her daughter she stopped teaching and began working for the Consumer Cooperative Association in Tokyo. 'When I was growing up,' she says, 'both my parents worked, so that set an example for me. I focused on food safety and worked on activities and proposals from the consumers' perspective. As a young mother I was concerned about food safety, which was the motivation for my involvement.' The work expanded her horizons. 'It was through this involvement that I first encountered social activism and became aware of the network of people actively concerned about food safety,' she acknowledges.

The issue of childcare was a challenge. 'This was especially difficult because at times both my husband and I were working outside the home. Childcare was a serious concern and caused much anxiety, but I was fortunate. When I was working with the Consumer Cooperative Association I was often able to bring my daughter with me,' she notes. This was because much of the work she was doing at that time centered on planning consumer social affairs activities and she could take her daughter to the planning meetings.

When asked about mentors and advice given she is clear: 'my husband is first on the list of those who encouraged and supported me. Nobuko Hiwasa is definitely number two on the list. There are also a number of close friends who provided mentorship and support. Most of these were women.' She has continued to follow in her mentors' footsteps to improve society. 'I wasn't looking for promotion or success,' she explains, 'I just wanted to improve society.' Interestingly, she was primarily motivated by John F. Kennedy's articulation of consumer rights in a speech he gave to the United States Congress on March 15, 1962.[1] 'Japanese consumer protective basic law, which passed in 1968, does not focus on consumer rights,' she notes, 'but governs and regulates business. It was not until 2004 that consumer rights legislation was enacted in Japan. Prior to that time, there was much unethical activity among producers in Japan.' She has spent her career advocating for consumer protections and, therefore, for companies to be more socially responsible.

Asked about her leadership style, Ms. Anan spoke about her role as Secretary General leading an agency with close to 300 staff members. 'Given the nature of the work,' she says, 'I asked all of them to think about their own situation and to identify the way they take care of their families and the concerns they have for them. Family should be one's first priority.' She believes that through sharing thoughts about care of and concern for family with co-workers new and creative ideas emerge. 'The second priority,' she says, 'is the consumers. The policies set forth should be based on and respond to consumer experiences. Asking employees to focus on their direct experiences assists them in responding positively to consumer needs and experience.'

She also believes it is important for the agency's employees to learn from daily activities, including the activities of local area consumers and consumer groups. 'This is essential to adopting a collaborative leadership style and teamwork throughout the organization,' she insists. 'There are nine sections in consumer affairs agency. In order to make sound and effective policies, it is essential to attend to all the sections.'

Ms. Anan sees many challenges in the future in the area of consumer rights and protection in Japan. 'First, Japanese consumers face many serious issues. While food safety is under control after the scandals in the first decade of the century, there is concern about fraud and scams targeting the elderly. Second, family relationships, the backbone of Japanese society in the last century, are not as strong as they were before World War II. Finally,' she continues, 'there are also problems that are a direct result of the Fukushima Daiichi nuclear disaster. These include responding to those whose lives and livelihoods are directly impacted by the radiation leaks. In addition, there is concern about the possible contamination of food and other consumer products that are produced in areas surrounding and downwind of the Fukushima power plant.'[2] She is confident that Japan's consumer movement will ensure appropriate responses.

For working women in Japan today, Ms. Anan is clear, 'childcare is still the major concern.' She notes this is no longer a concern for her; her daughter is grown and her husband now stays at home. 'This has made my life easier,' she says, 'but not all women have this luxury.' She believes that there has been some progress in terms of support for women and points to a few examples. 'There are some childcare opportunities that now exist either in the workplace or the neighborhood. The Consumer Cooperative Association subsidizes the cost of childcare for its employees. Also there are groups of volunteers who care for children. These volunteers receive small stipends plus expenses for travel and such. One area that still is problematic is income. 'Not only are incomes low, the gender wage gap still exists. However, expenses for education and childcare are high. Poverty rates, especially for single mothers, are very high,' she concludes. Finally, she notes the distinction between the way in which men respond to women and vice versa in management. 'They accept women as leaders if they are in strong positions,' she says, 'but lower management women employees are not as respected as those women in leadership roles.'

LEADERSHIP STYLE

Hisa Anan is a soft-spoken experienced leader who recognizes the challenges facing working women in Japan. By identifying with her staff and their personal as well as work-life situations, she exemplifies what Carol Gilligan (1972, 1982) called the caring dimension of women and how that caring can be an asset in an organization. She also identifies with consumers, and that too, exemplifies how managing for consumers and customers is often a characteristic of feminist leadership and good management policy.

NOTES

1. The rights enumerated in the speech to which Ms. Anan referred are as follows:
    (1) The right to safety – to be protected against the marketing of goods which are hazardous to health or life.
    (2) The right to be informed – to be protected against fraudulent, deceitful, or grossly misleading information, advertising, labeling, or other practices, and to be given the facts he needs to make an informed choice.
    (3) The right to choose – to be assured, wherever possible, access to a variety of products and services at competitive prices; and in those industries in which competition is not workable and Government regulation is substituted, an assurance of satisfactory quality and service at fair prices.
    (4) The right to be heard – to be assured that consumer interests will receive full and sympathetic consideration in the formulation of Government policy, and fair and expeditious treatment in its administrative tribunals (Kennedy, 1962).
2. In March 2011, a powerful earthquake and tsunami resulted in the meltdown of three reactors at the Fukushima Daiichi nuclear plant. Almost six years later, clean-up is still underway. The process is slow; reports indicate it will take 40 years or more to completely clean the site. Significant concerns continue to be raised about the impact of radiation contamination not just on food safety, the focus of Ms. Anan's life work, but also on the health of humans and animals and the environment in Japan as well as other parts of the world (Fackler and McDonald, 2011; Soble 2016).

6. Nobuko Hiwasa: Retired Independent Director, Megmilk Snow Brand Co., Ltd.

Ms. Nobuko Hiwasa was Independent Director at Megmilk Snow Brand Co., Ltd. between 2011, when the merger between Snow Brand Milk Products Co., Ltd. and Nippon Milk Community was finalized, and 2015 when she retired. Prior to the merger, she served as Independent Director in Snow Brand Milk Products Co., Ltd., a position she took up in 2002. Previously she worked with the Tokyo Consumers' Co-operative Union and Japanese Consumers' Co-operative Union. She also held the position of Secretary General of Shodanren, the National Liaison Committee of Consumer Organizations.

This is her story.

Two things in particular marked Ms. Hiwasa's childhood – moving from place to place because of her father's job and World War II. 'Both my father and my mother were born in the late 1800s, the turn of the century, during the Meiji era.[1] The environment in which my parents grew up was a very traditional, very conservative kind of culture. My father was born into a family of rice growers. His family did not own the land, but rented it in order to cultivate it. He was the eldest son and loved studying from an early age. He studied extremely hard; in the entire village he was respected as a person with very high talents. Because he was the eldest son of the family, it was taken for granted that he would be taking on the family business. Rather than taking over the family business of farming and rice-growing, he decided he would go to high school and then university. In those times,' she observes, 'the fact that he decided not to take over the family business was very unusual.'

When he finished university, Ms. Hiwasa's father joined the civil service and worked for the Ministry of Communication. 'We moved very frequently; once every two years or so he was given a new posting. Because we moved so frequently, it was very hard for me to make friends. I got accustomed to being on my own, doing everything on my own, being by myself,' she says.

'By far, the biggest event of my childhood was the Second World War. When I was in the first grade of elementary school, my father was mandated to serve in the military, but the administrative part of it, and was posted to Java, Indonesia. My mother's home was in Tokyo, so we went there. Eventually, elementary school children were not allowed to stay in Tokyo because the war was getting more fierce,' she recalls. 'I have two siblings, a younger brother and a younger sister, so my mother and we three siblings moved to Tokushima, a farming district which was my father's home.' The family moved twice more during the war eventually settling in her mother's home prefecture where relatives were living.

The war ended when Ms. Hiwasa was in fourth grade. After the war her father was a prisoner in Siberia for a year. When he got back to Japan he returned to his position at the Ministry of Post and Communication. 'That was the start of our post-war era life in Japan. At first we were in another prefecture but then we went to Hiroshima; it was only a few years after the nuclear bomb attack. I was in Hiroshima during my junior high school and the first grade of senior high school. When I was in the second grade of senior high school, my father was assigned to Tokyo so we moved back together. After high school, I went on to study in university here in Tokyo.'

'Growing up I decided I wanted to go to university but it was very rare for women; there were not a lot of girls who were studying. Most commonly,' she notes, 'women would graduate from senior high school and get married. In my days when they said university, they meant two-year junior colleges; after the women graduated they would get married. That was a common path. I entered the two-year course in the department of contemporary performing arts, but contemporary arts was what I wanted to study,' she declares, 'so I decided to transfer. I told my father that I wanted to go to another university, and he did not object. My father did not have this philosophy that women getting married early meant happiness for the woman. He worked very hard, he enjoyed working hard and studying hard so he was very supportive about that, and he felt,' continues Ms. Hiwasa, 'that if I wanted to study then I should study. I am very grateful to my father.'

Ms. Hiwasa believes parents have a significant effect on their children. 'My father, who encouraged my studies, was a great influence. Sometimes we forget the home is very important. An important thing is never to hear a father say, "No, you should not be doing that but rather doing this." My father would never say that to me. And my mother, too, was very open-minded; she never stressed the importance of a woman being married and going into the home right away. She was born into a family whose father was a rice wholesaler and she was the eldest daughter. Her family operated a very big wholesale business. Because the family was in commercial business they were relatively open minded in their philosophies,' she remarks. 'I learned from my parents how to be independent and have autonomy for my life and my decisions.'

Another person who had a great influence on her and was a role model was a professor at the Tokyo Woman's Christian University (TWCU). Professor Matsumura had this aspiration to be a professor, but she could not find a college that would accept women. There was only one that would accept a woman, so she was the only female student at the whole university. She told me when she was in classes she would never look up so she wouldn't have to make eye contact with anyone else. After she graduated she returned home to teach literature at TCWU. Her area of specialization was the Japanese traditional contemporary arts. She was single, not married. What she frequently said to me,' Ms. Hiwasa recalls, 'is that there is nothing you cannot do just because you're a woman. She told me to try not to rely on people, try not to depend on people, try to do things on my own; try to be autonomous, independent. She was extremely fashionable, very trendy. She would alter a costume to make a kimono for herself. Her ambiance was extremely admirable. She was a wonderful woman. I looked up to her, I thought how wonderful it would be if I could be like her. I was very much influenced by her.'

Ms. Hiwasa admits that rather than studying, she was very active in student activities, particularly the performing groups. 'I joined one that specialized in American works that were not being commercially performed. We students performed the works of Osborne and Eugene O'Neill. We introduced those works into Japan at the time. It was fascinating to decide on the cast, to produce, to rehearse; that whole process was fascinating,' she states. 'I was more interested in production than I was in the acting. We needed funding so of course we sold tickets for admission but that wasn't sufficient. That was around the time the private broadcasting business started in Japan, and there were part-time jobs at these private broadcasting stations. We got jobs at these stations in order to earn money. The money made working part time were the funds we used for our productions.

When it was time for me to graduate from university, I just happened to get married. The broadcasting stations kept calling me, even after I graduated, with job offerings. I had married at the time I graduated,' she adds, 'but I continued doing those part-time jobs, and that kept me quite busy actually. Then I became pregnant; the first job offer I received after I found out I was pregnant required me to be on a boat, shooting commercials on a lake. I turned it down; I quit the job, and I became a full-time housewife.'

She found staying home to be very isolating. 'I spent all my time with my child, and I felt like there was no connection with the outside world,' she recalls. 'There was a time where from morning to evening I would not even step out of the house. My husband, my partner, would do a lot of things for me including a lot of great work around the house. At that time, we had to walk to the post office to pay our phone bill, and he would do that for me, so sometimes I would not leave the house at all, and that was very stressful for me.'

Once her youngest turned three and began kindergarten, she was able to get out and try new things, one of which was to learn to swim. Eventually, she was invited to become a member of the consumer cooperative. 'At the time, their retail outlets stocked safe pork. They carefully monitored additives in the food and offered food items that did not have those additives. I was not really that interested in joining,' she acknowledges. 'When I was in university in 1960, the US-Japan security treaty was signed. The demonstrations objecting to the security treaty were a big deal. There was a major, major student movement to object to that. I was not interested in that very much. I was invited by friends to join, so I went one single time. I didn't think it was that important. People like me who were not really interested in that sort of thing were labeled "non-policy" students. So I did not have a keen interest in the cooperative movement, but my children were small; it made sense that I join the co-op, so I could secure safe food for them. My husband was a high school English teacher; by the time I joined the co-op I had two children, a boy and a girl.'

Her initial motivation for joining the co-op was simply to have access to safe food. In Japan there are networks of co-ops. There are local cooperative unions that are members of prefectural, or regional, unions as well as the Japanese Consumers' Co-operative Union (JCCU) to which local and regional cooperative unions belong. She had no intention of becoming an active member at any level and then one day she was asked to write a newsletter for the regional co-op group of which she was a member. 'I was a full-time homemaker at the time with a lot of time on my hands,' she admits, 'so I agreed.'

In time, the co-op developed a private label brand. The products were sourced from manufacturers who met their standards. 'On one occasion,' Ms. Hiwasa recounts, 'they wanted to have private label bakery items. I was asked to come aboard the team of co-op members who would go on bakery tours and screen bakeries to select which one we would place the order with. Members on the team would discuss, decide and select the bakery. It was a really rewarding experience to be delegated to make those decisions for the cooperative union. It was a very satisfying experience that expanded my activities because as part of the cooperative union, members would engage in a wide variety of advocacy and educational movements.'

In the 1980s, the cooperative unions in the region decided to integrate and consolidate which led to the establishment of Co-op Tokyo. Over time, Ms. Hiwasa became more active with the cooperatives and was appointed as a representative of the members to the Co-op Tokyo board. At the time, there were still some food additives whose safety had not been completely confirmed. The cooperative union publicized the risk of using such additives in order to abolish their use. In addition, it would also make appeals to the government and boards of food manufacturers requesting the abolishment of unsafe food additives. 'Our concerns were not just about food additives but other things like synthetic detergents that harm the earth. The mission was to be the voice of the consumers,' Ms. Hiwasa emphasizes. 'The main goal of the director at the national level was to initiate and oversee such advocacy movements. At the same time there were the voices of co-op members as well as consumers at large as to what types of products should be available at the cooperative stores. It was important to be conscious of these voices in setting direction or choosing the products to be developed.'

Ms. Hiwasa became increasingly involved with the co-op movements. 'At first, I sat on the board of Co-op Tokyo and then also on the board of the Tokyo Consumers' Co-operative Union or TCCU. TCCU is a union of both regional cooperative unions and a number of small unions. Because I was on the board of TCCU, I served on the board of JCCU. As a national organization,' she explains, 'JCCU serves the various cooperative unions by supplying products and doing research on safety issues to make sure co-op products meet all safety standards. As a board member, I would engage government cabinet members and visit the Ministry of Health, Labour and Welfare and the Ministry of Agriculture, Forestry and Fisheries to hold education sessions to enlighten cabinet members and to explain the activities of the JCCU to officials.'

'My involvement with cooperatives and consumer advocacy continued to grow,' she notes. 'In 1997, I became the Secretary General of Shodanren[2] that represents over 30 million consumers. After five years in that position I retired.'

The second part of Ms. Hiwasa's story is told in the third person based on a narrative developed by the authors in a series of cases on Snow Brand Milk Products (Werhane et al., 2010a, 2010b, 2010c).

At the time of Hiwasa's retirement from Shodanren, Snow Brand Milk Products Co., Ltd. (SBM) was reeling from the negative effects of two food safety scandals. Following the first scandal in the summer of 2000, the company, which had been the industry leader in Japan, had 'dropped off the Fortune Global 500 list, where in the previous year it had been ranked sixth in the industry behind Nestlé, Unilever, ConAgra, Sara Lee, and Groupe Danone' (Werhane et al., 2010a, 5). By the spring of 2002, for the second time in less than two years, the president and CEO and other senior officials were resigning in disgrace. One of the last things that Kohei Nishi – who was selected to lead the company and restore its reputation following the first scandal – did was to invite Nobuko Hiwasa to join the board of directors as an independent director to help reform and revitalization efforts.

The request was both unusual and quite unexpected. Hiwasa was not at all certain how she wanted to respond. Was the company sincere in wanting to reform and revitalize? Would she be accepted as an equal among the board members and would her views and suggestions be given serious consideration? Was the request publicity-driven? How would fellow consumer advocates view her if she accepted the position? What would the public at large, for whom she had worked for decades, think? (Werhane et al., 2010a, 1).

Analysts were clear that it would be extremely difficult for SBM to rebound from the back-to-back scandals. Its sales had plummeted, its credit rating had been lowered, its stock price had dropped 70 percent and, most significantly, consumer trust was almost non-existent. The odds of avoiding bankruptcy and turning the company around seemed low.

Unlike his predecessor, however, [Kohei Nishi] had put into place the foundation for a meaningful revitalization process – one that would put service to the consumer with trust and integrity at the center of all SBM activities. He believed that it was possible to revitalize the company, and he wanted Nobuko Hiwasa to be part of that process (Werhane et al., 2010a, 8).

After much consideration, she presented three conditions and made it clear she would only accept the appointment if they were met. They were as follows:

- Hiwasa had to have full disclosure of all activities and actions, even if this disclosure might seem to conflict with the company's immediate interests. Such disclosure was crucial if she were to be able to serve as a check on possible self-serving obfuscation, misrepresentation, or cover-ups by SBM employees.
- Hiwasa had to be completely free to comment and speak out as she saw fit—whether about the company or about Japanese corporate life in general—without interference from management. This freedom would include speaking directly with consumers, government officials, and the media.
- Management and other members of the board had to accept that she would be representing the interests of the customers (Werhane et al., 2010a, 10).

When she presented these conditions, she was quite clear about the consequences the company would face if they did not fulfill them or she determined that they were not serious about a turnaround. She would resign her position. 'Moreover, she reminded [them] that her years of consumer advocacy work had given her ready access to the media, so she would be in a good position to make public her reasons should she decide to resign' (Werhane et al., 2010a, 10).

> Assuming this role was quite a step for a woman who only a few months earlier had told the press that SBM was "the sort of company that deserves to go out of business." It was a clear sign that the company was serious about reform and revitalization (Werhane et al., 2010b, 1).

It was evident that the traditional, paternalistic, top-down Japanese management style had to be changed. 'The board, especially with Hiwasa's presence, recognized that a consumer-oriented, integrity-focused management style was crucial. It was also essential, as Hiwasa made clear, that the adoption of this new style had to be done with sincerity and integrity' (Werhane et al., 2010b, 2).

> In addition to becoming an external director of SBM, Ms. Hiwasa was invited to establish and chair a corporate ethics committee charged with preparing a revised code of conduct and establishing best practices in compliance and ethics throughout the company. She began by undertaking a listening tour of Snow Brand plants, laboratories, and sales facilities across the country. Initially, she had to prompt people to speak; the open town hall meetings were entirely unfamiliar to most employees in large Japanese corporations. Over time, however, employees began speaking freely as they realized that Hiwasa really wanted to hear their thoughts and that they would not be penalized, even when their comments about their immediate supervisors, SBM management, or the company in general were not positive.
>
> Hiwasa's success was due in part to her stature as a consumer advocate, but the fact that she undertook these visits on her own, without a management escort from headquarters, was also significant. According to Kohnose [president and CEO at the time], such solo trips by a board member of a Japanese corporation were unusual, but in his opinion, important, for they made it possible for her to "see the facts at each jobsite and bring back firsthand reports to the board." Not only did they provide input used to revise, refine, and continually improve policies and procedures, such trips also functioned as a system of

checks and balances to ensure that the information gathered by management through its established reporting lines was in sync with what Hiwasa saw and heard ...

As work on a revised code of conduct began, it soon became apparent that "many employees were unaware of the existence of the code of conduct." Hiwasa believed that this lack of awareness was directly related to the fact that the previous code had been prepared by a consulting company, not by SBM employees and management or consumers of the company's products, and had simply been promulgated from above. Consequently, even if people were aware of the code's existence, they had little, if any, commitment to it ... To avoid repeating these mistakes, those charged with the code revision consulted widely with a variety of stakeholder groups. Hiwasa alone interviewed almost 800 workers. The process took the better part of a year and included the rearticulation of the corporate philosophy or mission statement (Werhane et al., 2010b, 4–5).

Finally, in 2004 the new code of conduct was promulgated as a living rather than a static document. It was continually reviewed and in 2007 was rearticulated and reintroduced to all of SBM's employees. It was obvious that positive change was being effected in some areas. 'In a 2007 survey conducted by the Nippon Association of Consumer Specialists, SBM ranked in the top ten in each of three categories: "ethics-centered management (4), customer-oriented management (8), and disclosure of information (4)", (Werhane et al., 2010b, 7).

Following the efforts to revise the code of conduct, Hiwasa worked on strengthening the Corporate Social Responsibility functions at SBM. Following the merger with Nippon Milk Community, which was finalized in 2011, she was instrumental in assuring that the ethical institutional culture and practices supporting that culture continued in the newly designated Megmilk Snow Brand Co., Ltd. In June of 2015, Nobuko Hiwasa stepped down as an Independent Director of Megmilk Snow Brand Co., Ltd. She continues to be affiliated with the Yokohama City Consumers Association and to share her expertise with Japanese corporations such as Japan Tobacco Inc.

LEADERSHIP STYLE

Nobuko Hiwasa exemplifies principled leadership. In accepting the position at Snow Brand Milk she would not compromise the values of good management and quality products, a path she had followed in her previous directorships. That principled approach is a characteristic of both male and female leadership, but a characteristic that is not always evident in every leader. Ms. Hiwasa demonstrates that this approach can be successful, not only for character development but also in achieving worthwhile and profitable results for an organization.

NOTES

1. The Meiji era (1868–1912), often referred to as the Meiji Restoration, ended the Shogunate period and modernized Japan. This included modernization of the political system, through the creation of a constitutional government, and the economic system as well as changes in education and social attitudes. Unequal treaties that favored foreign powers by giving them privileges were revised and Japan became a world power. For more detail, see 'Meiji Restoration,' *Encyclopedia Britannica* available at https://www.britannica.com/event/Meiji-Restoration.
2. In English the Shodanren is known as the National Liaison Committee of Consumer Organizations.

7. Yukako Kurose: General Manager, CSR Planning Office, Teijin Ltd.

Ms. Kurose began her career at a department store. Passed over for promotions, she resigned. Today she is the General Manager for corporate social responsibility (CSR) planning at Teijin Ltd., a publicly traded Japanese firm with businesses in advanced fibers and composites, electric materials and performance polymer products as well as health care products and IT services. She is a respected advocate for women's rights in the workplace in Japan.

This is her story.

Ms. Kurose was university educated in industrial relations at Kyoto University. Her first job was at a Japanese department store working in public relations. It was 1986 – a year after Japan's equal opportunity law was enacted. 'However,' she says, 'when I became pregnant in 1992, I was passed over for promotion several times. It became more difficult when I had to leave work at 6:30 to pick up my daughter. I couldn't work later hours the way others did.' As a result, Ms. Kurose was assigned to an uninspiring clerical job that led her to resign in 2002.

'I began at Teijin in 2002 as a department manager,' she continued, 'and worked my way into upper middle management, first in human resources, then as a diversity officer. I was not trained as a leader or mentor. At the beginning of my career I lacked self-confidence and I found it hard to get feedback from the men.' Over time, she learned to brush off comments such as 'it would be better if you were a man' and has gained the confidence needed to advance in her career.

'At Teijin,' she explains, 'there is a focus on diversity and encouraging women and foreigners to accept positions.' The company has met with much success in the area of diversity, but as

Ms. Kurose observes, 'it took almost ten years to achieve this success. Part of the struggle was to change the mindsets of women who wanted to quit after having children.' Her own life story became a role model for career-minded women and she reports progress in changing mindsets.

However, it has not only been about changing attitudes. 'Efforts began small with an annual three-day diversity training program,' Ms. Kurose states. While these programs still continue, they are now supported by company policies that encourage women to continue in or return to their careers. In 2014 Ms. Kurose chaired an event focused on advancing women in the company, which is described in the company's 2014 CSR report. The event featured a panel that included diversity experts and women employees from Teijin. The stories which the Teijin women shared brought to life the positive impact that policies such as the childcare leave option have had on their ability to balance work-life responsibilities while maintaining successful careers (Teijin, 2014, 15–20). Ms. Kurose serves as a mentor to women at Teijin and is active in diversity efforts in Japan.

In addition to being a leader in the diversity movement, Ms. Kurose is senior in CSR planning at Teijin. More recently, she and Teijin colleagues co-authored the company's submission on best business practices in sustainability, which received the 2016 Eco-Balance Award for Best Business Practices (EcoBalance, 2016).

LEADERSHIP STYLE

Yukako Kurose is a positive-thinking leader. Her career exemplifies how what seem to be humble beginnings can develop into strong leadership if one is determined and committed. She responded to being sidelined in her first job not by seeing herself as a victim of the system. Rather she viewed it as a challenge and recreated herself as a diversity manager. She exemplifies the way in which a person can turn a negative outcome into a positive win-win.

8. Ryoko Nagata: Senior Vice President, Japan Tobacco Inc.

Ms. Ryoko Nagata is Senior Vice President and Chief CSR Officer at Japan Tobacco Inc., commonly known as JT. She has held numerous positions prior to that including Senior Vice President and Head of Soft Drink Business Division and Vice President Product Group, Food Business Division. Ms. Nagata is the highest-ranking woman at Japan Tobacco. She has been with the company for her entire career. She was educated at Waseda University in Tokyo and at the University of Florida.

This is her story.

'At university, I was a psychology major. I joined Japan Tobacco in 1987 soon after graduation. In 1986 the equal employment opportunity act had been enacted,' she explains, 'so I was hired as a general member of staff. Within the organization there was a very male-oriented culture, that of a very traditional Japanese company. Despite that I was able to take advantage of the fact that I was female and in the minority. Being a minority put me in a more advantageous position. I was given the liberty to do whatever I wanted to do.'

'There are two points that should be highlighted about the characteristic of the company,' she states. 'Originally JT was a government-owned organization. In 1985 it was privatized, that is, some shares in the company were sold to investors.[1] Beginning in 1994 JT was allowed by the government to be listed on various Japanese stock exchanges. It is considered a very progressive company and even has one woman on its board of directors.'

'The other characteristic of the company,' she continues, 'is it is the only cigarette manufacturer in Japan. Because it is the only Japanese company that engages in that industry, its competitors are all foreign companies. In order to be able to compete on the same playing field as the other companies we have to be very positive minded. And we have to be extremely proactive to ensure our diversity as a company.'

Ms. Nagata's first position was as a staff member in the cigarette sales office. 'I don't smoke,' she says, 'so I was not interested in cigarettes but was very interested in business. From day one I had declared my desire to work in a section other than the tobacco section. Because I did not know whether in the future my wish would come true, my first challenge was to work hard and do my best in the first section that I was posted to. I worked very hard in the cigarette sales office; after three months, I was transferred to the pharmaceutical division as the assistant sales manager of marketing.'

'With my psychology background from university, I was very good with numbers, with statistics and with numerical data. That led me to specialize in computer services. It was at the time companies were introducing office computers and systems,' she points out. 'JT needed talent in that area and human resources picked me. We utilized the computer system to compile various statistics that historically were calculated by hand. I ended up being on the ground floor of the change to computerized analysis of data throughout the whole company. I stayed in the pharmaceutical position for about three and a half years. During the time that I was part of the pharmaceutical team the concept of marketing was imported from the US to Japan,' Ms. Nagata recalls. 'With my academic background being psychology, I wanted to educate myself more about marketing and business so I applied for the company's study abroad program. I was given the opportunity to study at University of Florida. I was a "Gator" for two years.[2] I received a Master of Science degree in agricultural economics. I studied the basics of marketing, finance, accounting and trade but was more interested in the food business. At the time the food business was very, very small, almost non-existent; there was not even a business plan for the company to discuss.'

Upon returning to Japan Ms. Nagata was assigned to the human resources department. 'It is common for leading companies in Japan, publicly traded companies, to have training departments,' she notes, 'and I was given the responsibility to develop training programs and educate employees for the future of the company. I put together a sort of a mini MBA program. To our surprise, JT decided to enter the Burger King business in Japan. They were in it from 1996 to 2001.[3] This was the very first experience in my career having responsibility for opening a fast food restaurant chain. I was involved in the Burger King Japan joint venture from the very start.[4] Because I was in HR with responsibility for developing training programs I was given the responsibility to train Burger King staff. To prepare I went for a month to the Burger King training center in Singapore.'

JT had acquired the food products division of Asahi Chemical Company[5] and in 1999 Ms. Nagata was assigned to oversee product development for the frozen food division. 'This was a big change; I didn't know anything about frozen food. My subordinates were all from Asahi. We worked as a team, but the big challenge posed for me was that my direct reports were all men at the assistant manager level. They were very hostile,' she adds. 'The Asahi corporate culture was even more rigid, even more traditional than the JT culture. The fact that a young and female person had become their boss was something they could not stand. And I had to learn their business as well.'

'The only attitude that I could take on with them was to acknowledge and admit the fact that I did not know certain things and that I wanted them to teach me. Among the younger staff members,' Ms. Nagata observes, 'there was a very welcoming attitude about the fact that there was a female manager coming on board the team and becoming their boss because then the young staff members could hope for change.'

At the time JT made a number of acquisitions. 'These were different kinds of businesses which included the people within those organizations; it was like a melting pot of diversity from all over the world,' she recalls, 'not just in gender but in terms of age and culture as well. JT had to accommodate this diversity and was aware that they had to change and to change they had to be open minded. In being positive about diversity, they could not ignore the role of gender equality and had to be active in providing opportunities to women,' Ms. Nagata insists. 'Chances were to be provided with the new organization and those who had come from Asahi had to accept that JT corporate philosophy because they had to be working as a team to drive the business.'

'There were a lot of people who didn't like it. There was a certain group who were adapting themselves in order to be a part of the company; they wanted to change and adapt to the culture. But there were those who could not accept it and preferred a different world than JT. All they could do was leave the company,' she contends, 'and they did. It was younger people who were more adapting to the common culture, whereas others just could not accept it and could not adapt. It was not a continual outflow; we were finding those who had decided they would not fit made the decision within a year so there was this period of sorting out in the initial first year.'

'At the time I was assigned to be general managers of foods business in 1999, I was the first female to be posted to a management level position, not just in JT but among other Japanese companies as well. This was also the first experience at JT for a female who had experience studying abroad to become management,' she acknowledges. 'I was able to develop the business, grow the business, and we are happy to say we came up with some big products that drove the food business.'

'Then in 2008 it was the same story of being posted to a position where I had no experience, as the executive to lead the beverage business. I had no experience in beverages, so that was another first for me. I confronted a new set of challenges with the beverage business,' she admits. 'As general manager of the frozen foods business I had 50 people that reported to me. The beverage business was much bigger; I had 5000 employees. At the time, the level of sales in the food business was around ¥40 billion where the beverage business was something in the order of ¥180–200 billion. The most profitable part of the business was cigarettes,' she points out. 'In the cigarette business JT was a market leader in Japan with 60 percent of market share. The beverage market share was only 3 percent. Canned coffee was the main product along with Japanese tea, corn soup and hot orange citrus drinks; it is soft drinks only, no alcohol. The challenge was to look at the business, grow the business and expand the scale of the business to drive profitability.'

Ms. Nagata attributes some of her success to her leadership style. 'I think that my uniqueness is that I am positive minded. I hate losing. I like to be the first person to do something; I like being the first of a kind. I think I get along well with employees. Of course, I don't know all of them but generally speaking I am very easy to understand; I am an amicable person. That is how I am perceived to be within the company. There is one thing I have to be conscious and careful about, and that is not drawing a lot of attention to myself when talking with different people and communicating with different people. I want to be useful for my junior staff. I need to be careful not to convey the message, "I'm special," so the women don't think, "Oh she is special, I can't be like her." They can be special,' she insists, 'and that's the message I want to convey. The basic rule here is if there is a wall you have to confront, you have to either break it or overcome it.'

'For myself, my parents had a good understanding of me and my sense of values as well and they respected that. I am single. I have no children. I live with my mother, so it's just the two of us. As a child, I was told, "decide for yourself and once you make the decision and persevere, don't give up." It is in my generation that the trend started for gender equality, that women also had the opportunity to become professionals, to develop careers and work outside the home. In society at large, there was not as much resentment of Japanese women becoming professional and working outside the home.'

'Since there isn't a mentoring system at JT, I had to go and look for mentors myself,' she concedes. 'They were people who are respected and looked up to, my seniors. They were in the tobacco business or belonged to companies other than JT. There was nobody I could look to as a mentor in the food business, but I had a network of people to tap into to seek advice, mostly men.'

'At this point in time there are very few female management personnel within the organization but,' she adds, 'we are making steady progress. The number of new female graduates joining the company is increasing; they are 30 percent of new graduates joining the company. There is also a steady increase of women being posted to management positions. The basic thing is continuity. Continuity will bring its fruits. In Japan we frequently talk about the end of the curve. There is marriage; there is child rearing, particularly for women in their mid-thirties. As long as women can keep working through that time, through those events in their life, then that can bring change,' Ms. Nagata maintains.

There are other changes that she sees as well. 'Traditionally in Japan there was this concept of lifetime employment, of being loyal to the company and the company being loyal to you, but I think that philosophy within corporate Japan is dwindling. However, there is anxiety over the Japanese economy that is bringing about a great sense of valuing stability. It is a fact,' she declares, 'younger people are looking for stability. Japanese companies in general are looking to globalization, and in order to be successful, to survive, you have to be aggressive. There is a certain segment of the younger generation who cannot keep up with that pace. I think stability and comfort zone are contradictory to being aggressive; in order to be aggressive you have to take risks,' she asserts, 'and some young generation people cannot do that. I don't believe that applies to just JT but to any company in the global market.'

LEADERSHIP STYLE

Ryoko Nagata has broken all barriers for Japanese women. In many of the positions she has held, she has been the first woman to do so. However, like many women leaders, she is modest about her accomplishments. She exemplifies courage, risk-taking and perseverance and her team-building experiences are exemplary in Japanese management. Ms. Nagata serves as a role model for other Japanese women in the workplace.

NOTES

1. Japan Tobacco Inc. was established in 1985 as successor to Japan Tobacco and Salt Public Corporation which was a state-owned monopoly that was privatized through share offerings to investors. The government retains a 33 percent stake in the company (Japan Tobacco Inc., 2015a, 47).
2. The alligator is the mascot of University of Florida; students and alumni/ae are referred to as 'Gators.'
3. After a fierce price war with McDonald's, Burger King along with other competitors closed its operations and pulled out of the Japanese market in 2001.
4. In 1996, Japan Tobacco Inc. entered into a 50-50 joint venture with Grand Metropolitan PLC, a British conglomerate that owned Burger King at the time (Associated Press, 1996).
5. In 2001, the company was renamed Asahi Kasei Corporation.

9. Mieko Yoshida: Retired Executive Officer and General Manager of Quality Assurance Department, R&D and Quality Assurance Division, Nisshin Seifun Group Inc.

Ms. Yoshida spent her entire career at Nisshin Seifun Group Inc. (formerly Nisshin Flour Milling Company, Ltd.) beginning in the food research center in 1974. She rose through the company and was the first woman promoted to management and then in 2006 to Executive Officer of the company.

This is her story.

Ms. Yoshida graduated from the Department of Food and Nutrition at the Faculty of Human Science and Design at Japan Women's University in 1974. Despite the paucity of women in commerce at that time in Japan, Ms. Yoshida was determined to have a career in business.

'I was in high school when I thought to build a career. I came to believe that there is only one life, so you need to live it in full. Otherwise life will be useless. Fortunately, I was a good student at university. I studied various topics with a particular focus on food and nutrition. In 1974 Japanese companies were hiring women, but mostly in inferior positions,' she recounts. 'Women employees were not contributing to the company and its businesses. In food industry, it was men who developed the products, and women who bought the products. We were not sure that men were relating to their customers.'

While at university Ms. Yoshida decided she wanted to work in the food industry. 'I was interested in developing food that was safe and good. I researched the hiring practices of a number of Japanese food companies and found that Nisshin Flour Milling Company was hiring women into management positions. I accepted a position there. For 13 years, I worked in the food research center at Nisshin. Then I was transferred to the product development section of the food division in the head office where I eventually became Section Manager in charge of packaging. I was there for six years before being transferred back to the food research center to be the Section Manager of wet products. Wet products,' she explains, 'include products to which you add liquid, such as ramen noodles, or canned goods that are moistened, such as some pet foods. At Nisshin at that time we were manufacturing pasta and other foods and developing new packaging for all food products.'

In 2000 Japan experienced a major food contamination incident. 'That incident raised the legal requirements for food safety and my job changed to focus on product safety. However, in 1998 our company had begun to focus on food safety,' Ms. Yoshida recalls, 'so Nisshin was prepared for the new regulations. Four years later in 2004 I was promoted to General Manager of Quality at the Center for Research and Development and Quality Assurance at Nisshin, now part of the Nisshin Seifun Group, a holding company that was formed in 2001.'

'I had always thought I would remain in charge of product analysis and retire there,' she states, 'but at age 55 I was promoted to Executive Officer and General Manager of Quality Assurance of the same division. When I reached 60 years old in 2011, I was required by law to retire but I stayed for another year as a Corporate Advisor on quality assurance. I was able to work on things that had been left undone previously.'

In reflecting on her career, she admits there were many challenges. 'Balancing family, childcare and career was the greatest challenge. There was little available for private childcare in Japan at that time. In Japan we assume the mother will care for the children full-time. I worked one hour away from my daughter's school and could not get always get home for vaccinations, teacher meetings or other school events. Also,' she continues, 'I had no mentors because there were no women role models and few men who were supporting women at that time. I had a few working women friends with whom I networked informally, but I received little advice as I progressed through the company. Today at Nisshin about 30 percent of new hires are women. But there is only one female section manager and no senior managers.'

Ms. Yoshida also had to overcome gender stereotypes. 'Men have this belief that mothers should take care of children or children will fail. The Japanese government passed equal opportunity legislation in 2006. But other laws do not support women in the workplace. Men get a family allowance. Career women do not. Spousal benefits are federal. But different companies have different policies. In some companies men get low-cost company housing but women do not. Benefits are given to the head of household, and it is assumed that person is a male,' she observes. 'Also, with a stay-at-home wife the family has a lower tax rate and you can get social security benefits without paying into the system or ever working. So, these policies discourage women to work.'

'In addition,' she continues, 'companies often offer benefits for a stay-at-home wife and children, but not for working women. Working women have to pay for childcare; they are not given company housing so this is not equal treatment. If two managers earn the same gross income, and one is a woman, her net income will probably be about ¥20,000 less than her male counterpart.'

The stereotype of women goes beyond the belief that women should stay at home once they are married. 'Men unconsciously separate women from men and don't imagine women can be executives or even good managers,' she declares. 'Men don't think they are discriminating against women. All of this is subconscious. Men hire men, but this is often habitual or unintentional discrimination. Men help each other at work but not women so much unless they are ordered to. Men will correct their male colleagues but they won't correct their women colleagues. They don't work to promote women but claim they do. This makes promotion for women more difficult. I tried to make male managers become aware of this discrimination and looked to them for criticism, for what I as a manager needed to improve on. My only breakthrough,' she acknowledges, 'was to relate to male managers informally after hours to create bonds and trust.'

Another factor is Japan's traditional system of one-company, one-career. 'Most Japanese companies have lifetime employment and a strict seniority system, partly based on how long one has worked at that company,' Ms. Yoshida points out. 'Women who step out of the workplace to have children usually cannot get new full-time jobs after having children, or if they do, they never get executive positions. Also Japanese employees are rewarded for long hours even if they are not very capable. This is a challenge for women. There is a new movement of trying to evaluate performance, not hours, but this is still a "work in progress." Even so, there have been some changes in attitudes toward women in the workplace in Japan,' Ms. Yoshida acknowledges. 'It is only recently, but there is slowly gradual improvement. The slow pace is particularly troubling in the food industry because most of their consumers are women.'

Ms. Yoshida's family was very important to her career. 'I am married to someone who is a great supporter of women in the workplace. I have one child, a girl who is pursuing a career with a tire manufacturing company. My daughter tells me about the kinds of challenges there are in the workplace today. For example, if there are overseas jobs, men who are less capable than women are usually chosen. Still,' Ms. Yoshida concludes, 'as more women are working things will improve, so we need to encourage women to work outside the home.'

LEADERSHIP STYLE

Mieko Yoshida appears to have followed what Americans would call a typical career path, but in Japan this path is extraordinarily unusual for a woman, and she is an exemplar of what can be achieved despite discrimination and negative mindsets about women in the workplace. She is a courageous leader undaunted by what to most would appear to be impossible roadblocks. As a leader in food product development and safety and as a model of a married, smart and successful female executive she serves as a role model for young Japanese women entering business today.

PART III

Jordanian women leaders

Introduction: The Jordanian context

Though Jordan has one of the 'poorest economies in the Middle East, with 14 percent of Jordanians living below the poverty line,' it has one of the highest literacy rates in the region (United Nations Development Programme, 2012, 7). This reflects the access to education that primary school aged children have with 91 percent of all children attending primary school. Of these, 49 percent are girls and 51 percent are boys. While attendance drops at the university level where there is only a 31 percent attendance rate, it is interesting to note that the percentage rates of those women and men attending are reversed at 51.9 percent women and 49.1 percent men (United Nations Development Programme, 2012, 7). This reflects the government's investment in education which enabled Jordan 'to achieve its Millennium Development Goals (MDG) in education in 2005' (Al-Zoubi, 2014, 45). Despite such impressive success in education of women, they make up less than 16 percent of the workforce (International Finance Corporation, 2015, 17).

With such a low rate of female employment, it is not surprising that the World Bank found the rate of women's participation in top management positions in Jordan among 'some of the lowest in the world, even compared to other Middle Eastern countries' (International Finance Corporation, 2015, 17). In large measure this is because Jordanian women 'usually only work a few years prior to getting married, raising a family, and unceremoniously slipping out of working outside the home' (Cordes, 2015). Social and cultural pressures play a significant role in lack of women's participation in the workplace, as do structural barriers.

Some report 'negative perceptions of work carried out by women' (United Nations Development Programme, 2012, 3). Dr. Amid Abdelnour is not among them. He 'is convinced that women often deliver better outcomes than their male colleagues. Women are more focused and dedicated to the job. At least until they head [sic] the call of society's norms concerning marriage and family. He considers this a social problem' (Cordes, 2015). The World Bank finds deeply embedded gender roles 'reinforce the views that married women maintain the household while married men work, and that women, particularly married women, need to be protected from certain types of working conditions' (World Bank, 2013, 33). These social norms seem to be reflected in the imbalance in numbers of women employed across industries and economic sectors. For example, 'women (mostly the highly educated ones) [are concentrated] mostly in education (38.6%), human health and social services (12%) and public administration (12%)' (World Bank, 2013, 33). Such concentration in these civil service sectors is not surprising given that 85 percent of employed Jordanians are employed in the public sector (Barcucci and Mryyan, 2014, 8).

At the other end of the spectrum, 'only 3.9 percent of all entrepreneurs in Jordan' are women, a remarkably small percentage in a country where 'small and medium size enterprises (SMEs) constitute 95% of its economy' (Al-Zoubi, 2014, 45). In addition, 'it is estimated that three quarters of women's enterprises in Jordan are home-based' (Al-Zoubi, 2014, 52). These women-owned businesses tend to be small in scale, focus on local markets, and dominate certain service sectors such as beauty salons, florists and fashion boutiques.

In addition to social norms, which present challenges, women in Jordan also face structural barriers. Working environments are often not women friendly. One UN study noted:

> When the environment is hostile, such as situations in which women are harassed or abused at home for being late or in which there is no night transportation, or in which women assume the burden of domestic work, women themselves may withdraw and not come forward to access opportunities. This behaviour on the part of women is often interpreted as women exercising their choice or as women being incapable (United Nations Development Programme, 2012, 11).

Another barrier facing women, despite the successes they've made on the educational front, is the 'clear disconnect between the skills and education that women acquired and the skills requested by employers, particularly in the private sector' (World Bank, 2013, 11). Very few women pursue studies in science and technology that would provide them with skills that are in high demand, particularly in the private sector. From the World Bank's perspective 'female workers are not only locked into low growth sectors but also in sectors with low labor productivity, in particular education, health and public administration' (World Bank, 2013, 11). Women have to negotiate legal barriers as well. Among them are restrictions on nighttime employment, earlier mandatory retirement than men in some sectors, and differences in access to benefits, including pensions (World Bank, 2013, 14). If a woman is married, her husband has the right to deny her permission to work, unless there is a stipulation rescinding that right in the marriage contract (United Nations Development Programme, 2012, 12). Women seeking to be entrepreneurs confront regulatory barriers that can limit access to credit. In addition, they report unequal treatment on the part of financial institutions; collateral requirements for loans are often higher and husbands are asked to guarantee loans in the case of married women (World Bank, 2013, 57). More subtle barriers also exist. As the International Finance Corporation report *Gender Diversity in Jordan* notes, many documents, such as corporate governance codes, 'are nuanced with gender-biased language. Male terminology dominates all aspects of these codes' (International Finance Corporation, 2015, 15).

CHANGE ON THE HORIZON?

Strides are being made in a number of areas to attain gender equity in the workplace and beyond. Some are on the legislative front. Labor laws now require private companies to provide childcare facilities when more than 20 women have among them a minimum of ten children under the age of four (Cordes, 2015). Prior to 2013, women needed to have permission from their husbands in order to apply for a passport; this is no longer the case (Freedom House, 2015). As a way of undercutting gender specific social roles, there are calls to provide paternity leave in order to foster greater acceptance of men's responsibility for children and family (United Nations Development Programme, 2012).

Other indications of change are found in efforts to enhance women's leadership skills by organizations such as the Business and Professional Women Association – Amman, established in 1976; its mission is 'to open pathways and provide platforms for

Jordan's women to contribute to our national economy and society overall' (see http://bpwa-amman.org/About-Us/About-BPW-A). Regional organizations also have similar goals. These include the Middle East and North Africa Businesswomen's Network (MENA BWN) and the Arab International Women's Forum (AIWF). In 2012, the latter established the Young Arab Women Leaders: The Voice of the Future initiative and held the first annual conference in Amman, Jordan. As indicated at that conference the aim of the initiative is 'to assist a wide spectrum of young women leaders in Jordan and across the region to further optimise and strengthen their personal business skills and overall contribution to the business world and community at large' (Arab International Women's Forum, 2012). The initiative continues to bring together young women leaders from across the Middle East as part of the ongoing 'commitment of AIWF to achieving sustainable empowerment for women in the region' (Arab International Women's Forum, 2012).

Signs of positive change can also be found in the private sector as exemplified by three Jordanian companies: Biolab, a private medical laboratory group; Umniah Mobile Company; and Jordan Ahli Bank. They are among participants in a partnership between KVINFO, the Danish Centre for Research and Information on Gender, Equality and Diversity, and the Business Development Center (BDC), an Amman-based nonprofit committed to fostering economic development and public reform. A primary goal of the partnership is to foster employment opportunities for women in both the public and private sectors.

Biolab, along with Umniah and Jordan Ahli Bank, is involved in the Gender Sensitization Project, a program of the KVINFO and BDC partnership, that focuses on the adoption of human resource policies that promote recruitment and retention of women as well as advancement of women into senior leadership positions. Dr. Amid Abdelnour, CEO and the founder of Biolab, acknowledges a high turnover of women employees in the industry. Given that 60 percent of its employees are women, this is of particular concern for Biolab. Its retention strategies include flexible working hours, extended maternity leave and professional development activities, such as support for graduate level education (Cordes, 2015).

In addition to its collaboration with KVINFO and BDC, Umniah Mobile Company is also a participant in the gender diversity management initiative sponsored by GIZ, a German development organization; Umniah is one of seven companies in the region to sign cooperation agreements as part of the initiative and to institute family-friendly working conditions (Deutsche Gesellschaft für Internationale Zusammenarbeit, 2015). According to KVINFO, the company is leading 'a new trend in Jordan by working to reduce subjectivity in the recruitment process by subjecting all interested candidates to standardised evaluations and aptitude tests prior to job interviews' (Cordes, 2015). Creating a welcoming workplace environment for women is important on many levels, not least of which is the company's ability to continue to expand its business.

> The IT sector in particular needs more women employees in order to make up for the brain drain of talent to the neighbouring Gulf states due to higher salaries. According to Sami Jarrar [Director of Human Resources and Corporate Affairs], women tend to be more stable and loyal employees and are much less likely to try their luck working abroad (Cordes, 2015).

Umniah was named by *Jordan Business* as one of the top 20 companies to work for, in part because of its focus on corporate social responsibility (*Jordan Business*, 2015). In December 2015, the company announced it would be a signatory to the United Nations Global Women's Empowerment Principles (SAMENA Telecommunications Council, 2015).

At Jordan Ahli Bank, the oldest bank in Jordan, 42 percent of employees are women. The company has made a concerted effort to create a workplace that fosters gender diversity and equality by adopting measures that create a woman-friendly environment and address women's needs in terms of working hours and childcare as well as ongoing training and professional development. Not only does the bank work to empower its own women employees, it also established the Al Nashmeyat Initiative which:

> offers a wide variety of consultancy services that help female entrepreneurs secure more funding for their projects and improve their financial solvency, in addition to offering training activities on effective human resource management. The initiative also supports women residing in rural communities in achieving socioeconomic empowerment by building their capacities and reinforcing their participation in the production and exportation of local products (Jordan Ahli Bank, 2015).

While these various initiatives provide models for successfully improving employment opportunities for women, not all support this trend, as Mohammad Adwan of Jordan Ahli Bank acknowledged:

It may well be controversial for me as a man to support women's improved access to the labour market. You will definitely find conflicting views on this issue across the Middle Eastern countries. And the majority in Jordan does not necessarily concur with me – a change of opinion will require a fundamental change of mentality. But we have the power and opportunity to instigate change precisely because we are male (Cordes, 2015).

Noor Imam echoed this sentiment when addressing the first National Consultations on Gender Justice in Jordan held in August 2016; as reported in the *Jordan Times*, she said, 'Even if we have good laws, cultural constraints are still hindering gender justice in the region' (Azzeh, 2016).

10. Jumana Ghunaimat: Editor-in-Chief, *Al Ghad* Newspaper

Ms. Ghunaimat[1] is the first woman to be editor-in-chief of an Arabic daily newspaper in the Middle East. Prior to that appointment she was a deputy editor and head of the economic section of the newspaper. She studied at the University of Jordan where she earned a degree in political science. Before joining *Al Ghad*, she worked for a number of media outlets including *Al-Rai* Arabic daily newspaper, published by the Jordan Press Foundation, and as a freelance journalist and opinion writer. Considered a media leader in the region, she has participated in World Economic Forum events on the Middle East and North Africa and served as an outside expert for The Washington Institute for Near East Policy. She is a member of Jordanian chapter of the International Women's Forum.

This is her story.

'Before I was the editor-in-chief I was the manager of the economic section of *Al Ghad* newspaper,' Ms. Ghunaimat began. 'We are the first newspaper in Jordan. The elite and the educated in Jordan prefer to read *Al Ghad* than any other newspaper, so it's not easy but I'm managing it.' As a girl, she dreamt of being in journalism or politics. In 1995, she was hired by *Al-Rai*, an Arabic language newspaper published by the Jordan Press Foundation, in which the government has a majority share. At the time, it was top rated. As she notes, 'it used to be the first one in Jordan and it was a great opportunity not many people can get in their lives. I was at *Al-Rai* from 1995 until 2008; after that I came to *Al Ghad*. I spent four years as deputy editor-in-chief. In 2011, I was promoted to editor-in-chief. Everyone was very surprised. They said I was very young – I am not young even, I am 40. They said, "She's going to fail, she's going to take the newspaper to dangerous grounds." And I did [the latter].'

Jordan Media and Advertising Guide reports the paper has a circulation of 65,000, second largest after *Al-Rai* which has a circulation of 70,000 (Jordan Media Guide, 2017). According to Ms. Ghunaimat, 'One of the challenges in Jordan, which is a constitutional monarchy but with restrictions, is freedom of the press. I've been involved in many conflicts with police, government, parliament, defending our freedom as a journalist. That's why I said it was tough, this newspaper here.'

She's often asked how men respond to her as a woman in a leadership position. 'When they ask the men about me,' she says, 'they answer "we don't deal with Jumana as a female, we deal with her as an editor-in-chief." This is because I let them know me and who I am.' This approach is not new to her current position; she also adopted it when she was manager of the economic section. As she puts it, 'That was the first test, now it's the big test because I am the editor-in-chief. I have many dreams, many plans, to improve the newspaper, to make it regional; we are working on the website, on the new media – Twitter and Facebook. We've started to produce our own videos to make the journal more visible.' Her vision goes beyond media expansion and growing the website. 'We are thinking about an English version because it is important for the embassies and foreign people; the important issues we will translate and put online. It will help us to reflect our vision and mission and push for reform issues.'

When asked whether she thought that more women in leadership positions would help in Jordan, she replied, 'It depends on the kind of woman.' With only a few women in decision-making positions, she is concerned about the way the public perceives them. She's adamant, 'They have to choose the women carefully, they must be very qualified, they must not be in it for the prestige. If you choose qualified women who have good skills to affect society and let them make the decisions, then we might make a difference. If we just do it for prestige, for show or for numbers then that will never make change.'

As an example, she pointed to the quota system requiring that 15 seats in the lower house of parliament be reserved for women. 'We have 15 women in the parliament now, but that is because they still depend on the quota,' she said and noted, 'Some of them are weak and their political knowledge is very shallow, they need training. We still have many, many things to do and the road is still long. I think the mentality of many of the political decision-makers is such that they do not believe in women's skills or women's power to create change. They just think we need women in this position.'

When considering the role of the newspaper in working to improve the status and role of women, she is clear, 'We push for women's issues. We are trying to focus on the success stories; we are trying to focus on the economic contributions of women. This is an important figure. When we raise awareness that women share participation in the economy, it affects the political and social milieu, and everything will change.' She is insistent, 'Just give her an economic opportunity and it will change everything politically and socially.'

She brings her own style of hard work and dedication to her position as editor-in-chief. It differs from her predecessors' style she says, 'because I spend a long time here, I follow all the details, all the stories; I spend like 14 hours daily, maybe more, on the newspaper. This gives you different content, different teamwork style, and may, at the end of the day, give the reader a good project. A good newspaper reporter looks for something good to read, not just to print a story.'

She's received much support from an early age. 'My family, especially my dad and mom supported me very much. My mom is a teacher, my dad is a military man. I was studying engineering while I was in the university, but I believed this was not my passion. I decided to change to political theory and economics. When I finished my university, I began at *Al-Rai* and that was the beginning.' She continues, 'Now I am married with two children, a boy and a girl, and they support me. Working and being a wife and mom is hard and they help me very much. The children say, "mom you spend a lot of time at work." I tell them I have two choices, success and success.' Implicitly recognizing she is a role model for others, she tells them, 'I don't have the chance to fail or not to improve in my job. All the journalists, all the female journalists, are looking for me to make the tough decisions.' She sums up, 'It's all related even the social reform, to change women's positions, it's related, it's all social. Society, everything works together.'

POSTSCRIPT

Jumana Ghunaimat's dedication and resolve to promote change and fight to maintain freedom of the press are seen in her willingness to challenge that status quo. In September 2014, Ms. Ghunaimat wrote an opinion piece in *Al Ghad* in which she argued that some members of parliament were using their positions to benefit themselves rather than their constituents. According to reports, she:

> slammed deputies who take advantage of their positions to fulfill personal interests. "Some MPs claim to be fighting corruption, while they are deeply involved in corruption," she wrote. Some MPs, Ghneimat said, "give statements to the media that they are defenders of public money and of people's rights, while they are after securing some deal or getting some personal benefits" (Ghazal, 2014a).

As a result of the editorial a lawsuit was filed anonymously charging that she had violated the country's press laws. Among the charges, it was alleged that she did not seek the truth, was not being objective and had not acted professionally. She was also accused of defamation of an official entity.

Ms. Ghunaimat denied the charges. The Jordan Press Association voiced support for her; the president of the association said, 'We reject slander or defamation of any entity, but we believe this column falls within objective criticism' (Ghazal, 2014b). In late October 2014, the prosecutor general dismissed the case (Ghazal, 2014a). In a published message to the anonymous plaintiff, Ms. Ghunaimat not only thanked the many individuals and organizations that had supported her, but also pointed out that the decision 'champions freedom of expression and substantive criticism' (Ghunaimat, 2014).

LEADERSHIP STYLE

Jumana Ghunaimat exemplifies principled and courageous leadership in a country that is just beginning to recognize the strength of women as leaders. She mentors her staff by embedding those principles in all her reporters and editors. She is also a determined 'survivor,' undaunted by criticism and adversity. This determination is often exemplified in women during difficult challenges, but it is never easy. Ms. Ghunaimat is an illustration of that tenacity.

NOTE

1. Ghneimat is an alternate spelling that is sometimes used.

11. Reem Abu Hassan, JD: Attorney at Law

Reem Abu Hassan, an attorney at law, served in the cabinet of Prime Minister Abdullah Ensour as Minister of Social Development of the Hashemite Kingdom of Jordan from 2013 to 2016. Ms. Hassan is a long-time human rights activist focusing on family protection and women's empowerment. She served as Secretary General of the National Council for Family Affairs, which advocates for policies that support families, as President of the Jordanian Society for Protecting Victims of Family Violence and as a board member of the National Center for Human Rights. She is a founding member of International Women's Forum Jordan. She holds law degrees from University of Jordan and London School of Economics, University of London.

We interviewed Ms. Hassan prior to her cabinet appointment.

This is her story.

She began by stating that she was Secretary General of the National Council of Family Affairs (NCFA) and had been a practicing attorney for almost 20 years. 'The reason that I became a human rights activist,' she said, 'is because I worked for some time on issues related to domestic violence and child abuse. From that work I had the opportunity to lead the NCFA. I thought that would be a good phase, a new phase, in my life to actually work on public policy related to the issues that I believe in.'

She explained the role of the NCFA, noting it 'is a public institution funded by the government although it works as an umbrella for civil society. The NCFA coordinates family affairs for the government, as well as non-governmental organizations.' It also finds 'funders to work on sustaining and strengthening the family as a unit.'

Asked whether the focus of her work was mostly on public policy issues, she responded that 'there are public policy issues, but we believe in Jordan that the government cannot do everything on its own. There is a need for partnership with the private sector as well as civil society. Therefore, there was a need for an entity to coordinate the efforts and facilitate the discussions held between the government and other partners such as NGOs and other organizations.'

According to Ms. Hassan, 'Her Majesty, Queen Rania, believed that one of the ways to strengthen the rights of children as well as women is to work through the entity of the family.' She explains, 'The family is the basic unit of Jordanian society and although there are many bodies that work with children and women, there was no national body working with the family. The whole idea was to strengthen the unit of the family, because when you do that you are supporting the vulnerable members of the family mainly children, women and elderly.' She notes that the Queen is the chairperson of the Council's board of trustees, which also includes individuals from various ministries such as social development, Islamic planning affairs, and health as well as experts in the field of family and children. The intent 'is to have a strong board that can take decisions on issues related to institutionalizing policies as well as pushing forward reforms.' The emphasis is on analyzing legislation from the perspective of the family to determine whether it strengthens the family unit or weakens it. 'This is a new approach,' she remarks, 'because as we know many of the international conventions deal with the individual. But there are no international conventions that talk about the family as a unit. We identified certain legislation that would help towards strengthening the family unit.' One example she spoke of was work done to protect the rights of children who had been abused.

She began by speaking of the tribal tradition of *jaha* in which men who are considered the elders or representatives of a tribe speak on behalf of a family, for example when male elders meet to arrange a marriage. In the case of children's rights, the *jaha* can undermine the judicial system. The men, often from the same tribe or extended family, meet with the victim's family or guardian and arrange for them to sign a waiver of personal rights on behalf of the child. This usually resulted in either the reduction or setting aside of the perpetrator's penalty, or sentence, which not only undermines the courts and the legal system but also has the potential of once again placing the perpetrator in close proximity to the victim.

Ms. Hassan noted the NCFA found 'that because of social pressures, many families of molested children would waive their personal right when there was an attack on their child who is molested.' She continued, 'we advocated that the waiver of a personal right should not in any way constitute a reason to reduce a penalty, that any attack on childhood is an attack on what we call a public right, and therefore, the guardian or parent of that child does not have the right to waive a personal right.' It took a few years, but eventually the penal code was changed to reflect this positon. 'We're proud,' Ms. Hassan declares, 'to say that the reduction or waiver of that personal right does not constitute in any way a reason for the reduction of a penalty.'

She indicated that the process that resulted in the change involved working with 'some of the Islamic jurists because we have to go back to the fact that protection of childhood is the role of the state and nobody, no one, even the role of the legal guardian or parent can actually waive any of the rights of the child. This is a public right.' Asked about the role of Islamic law, Ms. Hassan was clear, 'Well, this is what Islamic law is. Children's rights cannot be waived by anyone because they are public rights. It's the duty of the state to protect and uphold the rights of the children. This waiver of personal rights itself was developed through tradition and tribal customs. And one of the reasons we were able to do this is because we were able to show that it does not have any basis to it in Islamic law.'

Whether it is advocacy for children, for women or for families, Ms. Hassan believes it is important to understand Islamic law and argues that all, including women, 'need to know so much more about Islam and the Islamic world [to] learn what the teachings allow.' She notes, 'the basic principle is that all things are permitted unless they are explicitly forbidden. If you look at political Islam one of the ways to actually control the people is for people to think that everything is forbidden unless such groups allow it. I think this is a way to control the masses,' she concludes.

From her perspective, 'it is the role of any educated person, not just women or men, to really help in pushing people towards knowing more about Islam and using Islamic arguments in the daily dialogue towards knowing about basic human rights. We need to know more about our own religion in order for us to protect our lives as human beings. One of the things we learn as children is that we are God's guardians on this Earth and to be worthy you have to be educated, accept others as they are. I think it's the same everywhere. I keep telling my children. You are God's guardians on this Earth; we all are, so it's our duty to learn and work and to be able to communicate with other people, otherwise we are not worthy of that gift.' She acknowledges, however, 'what is frustrating me now is that I find that the younger generation is more willing to accept political Islam as it is portrayed to them than trying to go against it because it frightens them. So we have these two sides. Either they do not want to deal with this one way or another or they are completely withdrawn.'

Reflecting on her career path, she states, 'the first thing to say is that I come from a family who are all into business. I am the first one who decided to study law. My mother could not accept the fact that I wanted to go to law school. I actually had the support of my father, though my mom was convinced when I explained that I would like to be able to speak my own words and make my own decisions. When I entered law school in Jordan it was very new; we were the fourth class for the law school. I was interested in corporate law – that was the family background. I was fortunate to meet a famous lawyer who mentored me while I was in school. When I wanted to go do my LLM in England I wanted to study constitutional law, criminal law, human rights. But he told me, no, you are going to study the subjects you need a tutor in, these other subjects you will get them by reading books and becoming a lawyer. I listened to him and I studied transnational enterprises, arbitration, international economic law and Islamic commercial law.' When she returned to Jordan, she interned in her mentor's office. Though he was a well-known corporate attorney, he also did pro bono work defending people's rights. 'He taught me that this is the responsibility of anyone who is an attorney, even if you are a corporate attorney.'

When she returned to Jordan in 1992 after living for a time in the United States with her husband, who is also an attorney, she decided not to work in his family's firm. 'My husband is very, very supportive of my work,' she says, but 'I decided it was better if I have my own law office with a friend of mine so that people will know me as Reem. And we started doing litigation especially for commercial cases which I love, being a litigator.'

This was at the time that Jordan was beginning to prepare for the Fourth World Conference on Women in Beijing, which was held in 1995. Ms. Hassan was asked to join a group of lawyers charged with reviewing legislation that allegedly discriminated against women. She agreed to join the group. 'I started with the idea that we were taught in law school that Article 6 in the Constitution says that all Jordanians are equal. I was asked to review the penal code because I was interested in that subject. That is when I started pinpointing and highlighting the discrimination against women in the penal code,' she states. 'At that time Jordan, for many reasons not to be discussed now, was labeled the hub of honor killings. The legal text was there in the penal code. That is when I decided to educate myself on honor killings. I collected and read all the court rulings dealing with honor killings from the 1950s to 1993.'

Her research led her to conclude 'that these cases do not happen by accident. There was no fit of fury as the legal provision stipulates. Some of them are premeditated, and that there is some kind of consensus among family members to do that, because of different reasons. One of them was the inheritance issue.' She also found 'that the perpetrator in almost all these cases is the brother, not the husband, and the younger the brother the better it is, because he will get a leaner sentence.' She makes it clear 'that this practice is completely away from Islamic teachings. In Islam there is no defense of honor killings.' Referencing a colleague who examined the sections of the penal code that mention exonerating and extenuating circumstances related to honor killings, Ms. Hassan says, 'it turned out that these were derived from the Syrian and Lebanese penal codes, which were derived from the French penal code. Honor killings have nothing to do with Islam.' Over her long career, she has continued to address this and other issues affecting families, women and children particularly through work on reform of the legal system and penal codes.

Her attitudes on leadership provide the key to her success. For her, 'one of the important things is actually to work as a team. I do not believe that anyone can lead a movement if he or she thinks they have the final word. I think having a team and learning from your co-workers is as important. The other thing is to be well informed; when you as a leader are in a meeting be sure that you have an opinion, that you are not merely "decor." A woman has to study a lot, to learn a lot, to know what's going on around the world, and be able to filter that and portray that to the co-workers.' She believes 'it's also important to know where people are coming from, what makes them tick, and what actually makes people motivated. I know financial reward is considered a motivation, but people also need to be recognized for what they contribute and have to offer an organization. Also, it is important to share, especially if there is a need to share in something dealing with their children, or giving advice, or taking advice. When I look at myself with my co-workers, I always like to think I am part of the team; when I am working with government or with institutions I always like to portray the fact that I am a serious woman. In many cases, the first thing the government official would want to think is that because she is a woman, she has no professional capabilities. And the third thing is governance and transparency; if co-workers feel that the woman is fair, and they tend to think women are fair, then they are ready to cooperate.'

She's optimistic about the future for women leaders, and not just in Jordan. 'I think the number of women leaders all over the world will be increasing, because I think that the leadership style of women is what the world needs right now – more compassion, more transparency and more understanding as well as close ties with the community.'

LEADERSHIP STYLE

Reem Abu Hassan has demonstrated purposeful, diplomatic leadership throughout her career. Without sacrificing her principles or the causes she has defended, she has achieved success working within the parameters of Jordanian law. This subtle but determined leadership has achieved miraculous results. There is much to be learned from this approach.

12. Nadia Shamroukh: Chairwoman, Jordanian Women's Union

Nadia Shamroukh, a former schoolteacher, trained as a lawyer. From 1990 until 2002 she worked as a volunteer at the Jordanian Women's Union (JWU), Amman, Jordan. In 2002 she was appointed General Manager of the JWU, a full-time position she continues to hold.

The interview with Ms. Shamroukh was conducted at the Jordanian Women's Union in Amman during a tour of the premises. There were several interruptions – cases and incidents that required Ms. Shamroukh's immediate personal attention. As a result what follows is based on her personal comments, what was gleaned from the visit and public sources.

This is her story.

JWU was founded in 1945 to focus on advocacy for women's rights in Jordan. Over time, its work expanded. In 1996 it opened a hotline providing a resource for battered women. This was followed in 1999 by the opening of the first shelter for battered women in the Middle East. As Ms. Shamroukh notes, this was not an easy task. 'When we started some of the people at JWU were against making it into a shelter. But when I meet women we have protected I am satisfied we did this. And some of these women we have helped now work with us on our projects.'

Today, among other things, JWU deals with acrimonious divorces and with so-called honor crimes – actions of women that are perceived as tarnishing or otherwise damaging the family's honor – which can put a woman at great risk of abuse or even death. JWU also works with police to assist women who have been trafficked. In addition, it provides children with protection, counseling and rehabilitation services. The clients served are not only Jordanian women but also Palestinian and Syrian women in the many refugee camps in the country as well as a few men. Though it is seldom that men seek assistance for abuse, JWU aids in those cases as well. Overseeing the many aspects of JWU's work is a daunting task. As Ms. Shamroukh states, 'Sometimes I feel that I would like to be a volunteer again. To manage all these programs, 15 locations and 150 persons is not the problem. The main problem is to find the funding for the programs.'

As with many shelters, those operated by JWU provide education and training for the women. The underlying philosophy is clear; providing women with the ability to be independent and enhance the quality of their lives, enhances the quality of civil society. It is important to understand that JWU's shelters and services are operated in a way that responds to the particularities of local customs and law.

Unlike many women's shelters in Western Europe and America that only work with abused women, JWU's shelters work with the abuser and the extended families of both the abuser and the abused woman. Because families are so close and often exert great influence on family members and because there are few laws protecting women from abuse, working with extended families is, in many cases, the only viable option. In some cases, where the families are at odds with the women or with each other, JWU's lawyers will appeal to the courts to protect the women.

Ms. Shamroukh prefers not to work with abusers, or persecutors as she calls them. 'But,' she is clear, 'I have to, because I have lists of lawyers who protect the persecutor.' Often the task is to overcome social customs and traditions that result in not understanding or disregarding the risks and dangers that face abused women. In some cases, this task is made more difficult by Jordanian guardianship laws.

For example, Jordan's Personal Status Law, which was amended in 2010, grants fathers sole legal guardianship over daughters until they have reached the age of 30, even if they are married. The father can insist the woman returns home, returns to an abusive environment. 'The daughter has to obey until she is 30,' Ms. Shamroukh said. 'That means that I have to deal with the father.'

It is complicated. 'If the husband is trying to find the wife [and goes to the police] they don't force the wife to go back to the husband.' If the father makes the request, 'the police, if they find her, try to convince her to go back to the family.' This is one of the reasons that JWU works with the extended family to help them understand the situation and ask for their assistance in stopping the abuse and helping the abuser to reform.

There are, of course, times where women refuse to return to home, often because they fear for their safety. They may feel threatened by their husbands or other family members, including siblings, and fear they will become victims of so-called 'honor killings.' Until recently these women have been put into protective custody. As Ms. Shamroukh notes, 'If a woman refused to go back to her husband, the only option was jail, to protect her from the family. If she's threatened, if the police feel that she is threatened by the family, they kept her in jail.' She is pleased that the government has opened a shelter for such women.

She is adamant, 'part of our mission is to keep battered wives and daughters at the shelter. We deal with thousands of cases, but to date no one has been killed. No one from our cases was killed because, when a woman is out of the house and comes to us, we call the family. We explain that she is in the Union with other women.' This not only maintains the woman's respectability, but also provides an opportunity to begin working with the extended family.

In some cases, the root of the problem is not the husband. 'Some men are under the pressure of their family, and everyone seems to interfere in their lives. I remember a time I had a man in the office; he was shouting, shouting, "I want to go to the police against my woman because she was pregnant, she had the baby and she came here with the baby." The problem was between the families, the two mothers, not with the man and woman. The only thing we did was to stop the interfering.' It took a year, but the husband and wife were reconciled.

There is a recognition that 'men need help as well, because they don't know the law. When a man comes here, he is afraid, and he usually promises to stop abusing his wife. We get him to sign a paper agreeing to discontinue the abuse. Often the men think that this paper is a legal form.' She is clear, however, that there is nothing legally binding about the form. They also make certain the abuser knows that they have and retain doctors' reports. 'We discuss the report with the women, and we recommend that if they go to court they take the report. She, the woman, decides, we don't decide on behalf of her, we give her options and she decides.'

JWU encourages the women whom it serves to continue their education, to develop skills so that they are able to support themselves and any children they may have. She spoke of a woman who returned to say, 'You saved me.' Referencing the various workshops and programs, she says, 'We try our best to do something, and when someone tells you this it feels good. We empowered her to start at the university and now she's doing her MA. She was in one of our workshops, and I told her, "Why don't you continue your studies?" I don't remember saying that, but she told me that from being in the workshop, she started to believe that she could manage alone. We had hired her as a secretary while she was studying in the university. She finished the university, and she became an executive secretary. Now she's doing her MA in conflict resolution. Another woman working here now is studying accounting, and another one became a nurse. It is for this reason I continue.'

The JWU also sponsors a program for divorced and separated families by providing the space in which fathers can visit with their children. She recounts the story of one of the men. 'When he came to us he was young. He was divorced, so he came to see his child. He told me that when he came the first time, he was afraid to come into the women's place. Now he is retired from his job, he studied social work, and as a social worker at JWU he helps other families.'

Each case is different, so there is an action plan for each person. This will include the abuser. 'Men are abused as well,' she claims. 'So we need to liberate the society not just women. Men are under the pressure of poverty and ignorance. When you deal with men you feel that sometimes the man, even if he is the abuser, becomes the case.' She continues, 'We also decide if an abuser is violent or if he needs a doctor; if he seems mentally unstable, we send him to a psychiatrist.' She reports in the majority of cases the mindsets of the men with whom they work are changed. 'Still many men believe that in our society women are the slaves,' she acknowledges. It is this that spurs JWU's advocacy work. She is explicit, 'We have another focus. We work in parallel on changing the laws, to amend the laws, especially the family law, which is against women and against children.'

Of course, funding is needed to support the various activities with which JWU is involved. 'The Jordanian government doesn't give us anything, and we don't want anything because we want to be independent and to continue as an independent organization. We don't want anyone to require us to follow conservative strategies.' Funding comes from other sources, including 'Swedish NGOs, Danish NGOs and the Spanish, but the Spanish stopped after the [2008] financial crisis. There are also Italian NGOs; they are our partners. We also get funding from UN agencies – UN women[1] and UN FBA[2] – and the European Union and donations and membership fees from our members.'

When asked about contributions from Jordanians, she explains that most of those funds come from staff contributions. NGOs often set salaries according to standards in other countries. She and other staff members choose to donate a portion of their earnings to the JWU. She's quite clear, 'the donors know this. I tell them all the time, "You want us to take high salaries, okay." So I ask for the high salary. We are poor people, but a rich organization; we are proud of this. The value is in the work, not the money.'

Employees do leave for higher paying positions. After a few years, some employees return even though it means a significant drop in salary. She mentions a colleague who came back after working for a foreign NGO. At JWU she's earning 40 percent of what she earned at the NGO but she's happier. Ms. Shamroukh is emphatic, 'The people who work here have to be believers and be willing to struggle, struggle to work on women's issues and women's liberation; you have to be like this. If they aren't they can't work in this situation.'

LEADERSHIP STYLE

Nadia Shamroukh is in some sense an accidental leader. Starting as a schoolteacher she found herself unable to ignore the plight of women's rights and family abuse in Jordan. While never seeking publicity, she has worked tirelessly for women's rights and the protection of women from family abuse and trafficking. Ms. Shamroukh is also a situational leader. She manages her ideas about abuse with an approach that matches the cultural mores of most Jordanian extended families, with a model for approaching abuse that is specifically Jordanian. In a global economy, a situational approach is critical for success in different cultural climates.

NOTES

1. 'UN women' refers to the United Nations Commission on the Status of Women.
2. Folke Bernadotte Academy (FBA) is a Swedish government agency for peace, security and development that often partners with the United Nations. According to its website, 'FBA supports international peace operations and international development cooperation. The agency conducts training, research and method development in order to strengthen peacebuilding and statebuilding in conflict and post-conflict countries. We also recruit civilian personnel and expertise for peace operations and election observation missions led by the EU, UN and OSCE. The agency is named after Count Folke Bernadotte, the first UN mediator' (Folke Bernadotte Academy, 2016).

PART IV

United Kingdom women leaders

Introduction: The United Kingdom context

For more than 40 years, the number of women in the workforce in the United Kingdom (UK) has been steadily rising. Two-thirds of women aged 16–64 are working according to a 2016 Catalyst report. Representing 46 percent of the workforce, this is the largest number ever, up from 53 percent in 1971 (Catalyst, 2016). Despite this increase and 73 percent of the population agreeing that gender equality is good for the economy (Olchawski, 2016, 6), the gender pay gap remains, with women earning on average 20 percent less than men (Catalyst, 2016). A recent Fawcett Society report notes 56 percent of men and 68 percent of women 'believe more needs to be done to achieve equality' (Olchawski, 2016, 8). However, when considering their own interests, only 47 percent of respondents indicate they would benefit from gender equality. Asked about men in senior positions making room for women, '60% of people believe that men in top jobs won't make room for women unless they have to' (Olchawski, 2016, 9). Also worrying is the perspective of those responsible for recruitment. 'A quarter of recruitment decision makers believe that a more equal society would not be better for the economy as compared to 9% not involved in recruitment decision making' (Olchawski, 2016, 6).

Despite these concerns, it is important to acknowledge the progress made at the board level of FTSE 100 companies in successfully meeting the challenge set forth by the government in 2011 to increase representation of women on FTSE 100 boards to 25 percent by the end of 2015 (Lord Davies of Abersoch, Steering Committee, 2011). The challenge, which was part of the Women on Boards initiative spearheaded by Lord Davies of Abersoch, was in response to a European Union Directive calling for greater gender diversity on corporate boards. Unlike European countries that responded by legislating quotas, the UK adopted a strictly voluntary scheme, albeit one with explicit target metrics. The success goes beyond the FTSE 100, with only 23 companies in the FTSE 350 still having all male boards at the time of the 2015 annual review report (Lord Davies of Abersoch, Steering Committee, 2015). This success, however, was accomplished largely through appointment of non-executive directors with the number rising from 117 to 239 women serving in that capacity. In contrast, the number of women executive directors rose from 18 to 24. This represents only 8.6 percent of executive directors of FTSE 100 companies. The number of women chief executives remained unchanged at five, with the number of women chairs at three, an increase of only one woman. These numbers reflect the low numbers of women in the executive pipeline. As Lord Davies noted, 'Boards are getting fixed, now we have to fix the low number of women Chairs and Executive Directors on boards and the loss of talented, senior women from the Executive pipeline' (Lord Davies of Abersoch, Steering Committee, 2015).

It would appear that the glass ceiling is still very much intact in the UK. In a survey of 3000 of its members, the Institute of Leadership and Management (ILM) found 73 percent of women but only 38 percent of men believe that the glass ceiling exists (Institute of Leadership and Management, 2011, 4). There are those, however, who believe the concept of the glass ceiling suggests that there is a single barrier for women to overcome and, therefore, does not account for the complex of barriers that women face and that inhibit their movement through the executive pipeline. Stefan Stern is among those who argue, 'women face a labyrinth, not just a ceiling in their quest for career success' (Stern, 2015).

Some of the barriers women in the UK face are common to women in other parts of the world. Among these are negotiating work-life balance, including primary responsibility for childcare, high cost of childcare and difficulty in negotiating a successful return to a career track following breaks. They also face gender bias. For example, research shows:

> that men's CVs are viewed more favourably by employers than identical CVs submitted by female applicants. Employers also have a tendency to recruit in their own image, and with the majority of top jobs being held by middle aged, Caucasian men this can only continue the cycle of inequality (de Valk, 2014).

In addition, many more positions held by women at senior levels are in functional areas, such as human resources, public relations and marketing rather than operational areas, such as chief executive officer, chief financial officer and chief operating officer (Sealy et al., 2016, 31). Lack of experience in operational areas makes it more difficult to gain an executive board position.

There is also the problem of 'glass borders.' It is fairly well established that an international posting is an important step for advancing into senior managerial positions, yet 'eight out of ten people posted overseas are men as organisations tend to discount women as strong candidates for those international assignments ...' (Lamb, 2013). The research also indicates that men are 'promoted on their potential – and actively pursue opportunities overseas, while women are promoted on their performance – and are much less likely to put their name forward for promotion abroad' (Lamb, 2013).

This tendency to avoid self-promotion is not limited to consideration of overseas assignments. According to the ILM report cited earlier, research shows that women are more cautious than men in applying for jobs or promotions. Men are more willing to put themselves forward for roles where they don't fully meet the criteria – 20 percent of men will apply if they only partially meet a job description, compared to 14 percent of women. Women prefer to play safe – 85 percent of women would only apply if they met the job description 'fully' or 'pretty well.' This reluctance to put themselves forward for stretching roles, thereby missing out on opportunities, is likely to prove career limiting (Institute of Leadership and Management, 2011, 6).

Women leaders are continually balancing accepted – and often expected – feminine traits with more masculine traits associated with positions of authority and power. This leaves them in a double bind; on the one hand when exhibiting feminine traits, they are perceived as soft or emotionally unsuited for leadership positions, and on the other hand when exhibiting more masculine traits, they are perceived to be too assertive or aggressive. It is not just men that have these perceptions. As Mavin et al. point out, 'the gendered nature of organizational contexts means that women, as well as men, hold women accountable to normative gendered expectations' (Mavin et al., 2014, 441). They note that 'the masculine symbolic order shapes and constrains women elite leaders' social relations with other women' (Mavin et al., 2014, 439). This can lead to tensions between and among women leaders as well as those women aspiring to leadership positions; these 'negative intra-gender relations' can hamper women's progress, especially at senior levels (Mavin et al., 2014, 439).

Added to the barriers uniquely facing women in the UK is the class ceiling. Of all adults in professional employment today, earnings are higher for those whose parents were also in professional employment. The finding that income persistence between parents and children has increased is not just a matter of those from privileged backgrounds getting a greater share of top jobs. Even when those from working-class backgrounds get professional jobs, they are likely to earn less than their colleagues who started off in professional families (Social Mobility and Child Poverty Commission, 2015).

Many factors are at play here including economic capital, cultural capital, which includes educational background, social capital, and even stereotypes based on a person's accent.[1] While the social mobility report indicates that working-class women have made advances in employment and wages to the point of achieving income parity with their male counterparts, it is clear 'that those born in working-class families face challenges in breaking through the class ceiling to professional work' (Social Mobility and Child Poverty Commission, 2015). This places an additional burden on some women trying to be part of the executive pipeline.

CHANGE ON THE HORIZON?

As noted in the Davies Review, the UK continues to be 'committed to a voluntary, business-led' approach to successfully advancing the role of women in senior management as well as executive level positions (Lord Davies of Abersoch, Steering Committee, 2015). To that end, target goals have been set and various initiatives put in place including having women hold 33 percent of appointments to FTSE 100 boards by 2020. Among other initiatives is the '25 by 25' campaign sponsored by Egon Zehnder UK, a professional services company engaged in executive search and talent advisory services; the goal of the campaign is to have 25 women as CEOs of FTSE 100 companies by 2025. A similar scheme sponsored by the

Introduction: the United Kingdom context 111

Department of Energy and Climate Change's POWERful Women (PfW) has set 2030 as the target date by which women will hold 30 percent of executive board seats and 40 percent of senior management positions in the top 100 energy companies in the UK (PricewaterhouseCoopers, 2015). There is also the Think, Act, Report initiative sponsored by the Government Equalities Office; the framework for this voluntary initiative asks signatories to pledge to 'Think: identify any issues around gender equality; Act: take action to fix those issues; Report: on how your business ensures gender equality' (Government Equalities Office, 2015). The three elements common to these and other initiatives 'are focused public attention; committed leadership; and corporate transparency' (Lord Davies of Abersoch, Steering Committee, 2015).

There are other signs of change on the horizon as well. In 2014 the government changed parental leave rules to enable parents to share up to 50 weeks of leave after the birth or adoption of a child and add some flexibility around newborn care; the amount of time that can be shared depends on the amount of time a woman takes for her maternity leave. For those not opting for parental leave, the maternity leave policy remains. A woman will receive 90 percent of her average before tax weekly earnings the first six weeks of her leave. Subsequently, she receives either 90 percent of her pre-tax average weekly earnings or £139.58, whichever is lower. It should be noted that this is the minimum statutory pay and companies are free to have maternity leave policies that are more generous. Employees also have the right to request flexible work arrangements. Employers must consider the requests but can refuse such requests for business reasons such as the inability to meet customer demand or to reorganize workload among other employees.[2] While these are positive measures, it is unclear how far they will go to retain talented women who are on track to move in to more senior positions.

The same can be said about the efforts being made to identify women with potential for C-suite executive positions as well as board appointments. Among these efforts are conferences for women identified by a board chair or CEO as having the potential for holding both executive and board positions. There are also efforts to provide coaching, mentoring and networking opportunities. Hopefully, women have been integral to planning these opportunities. As the RSA Group report indicates, 'Senior management needs to listen to what women say rather than simply providing a solution from a male perspective. For example, our study shows that women want pro-active mentoring and coaching together with commitment and endorsement from company leadership, rather than simply greater flexible working practices' (RSA Group, 2012, 3). While these many efforts are to be applauded, it remains to be seen whether they will overcome the hesitancy to self-promote that most studies identified as a hindrance to advancing into senior leadership roles. As de Valk argues, 'female leadership development needs to be subtle and must connect women's sense of identity as leaders to what motivates them' (de Valk, 2014).

NOTES

1. In addition to the Social Mobility and Child Poverty Commission Report, for a fuller discussion of the class ceiling see Friedman et al. (2015). Also see Workman (2015).
2. More information is available at https://www.gov.uk/browse/employing-people/time-off for complete details of leave policies.

13. Terrie Alafat, CBE: Chief Executive, Chartered Institute of Housing

In April 2015 Ms. Alafat joined the Chartered Institute of Housing, an independent nonprofit British organization, which is the professional body for housing in the UK and works in a number of other countries across the world. It plays a key role influencing policy to improve housing and communities for all UK citizens. Prior to that she served as Director of Housing in the Department for Communities and Local Government. She has worked in the British Civil Service since 2003, covering various housing policies including homelessness, affordable housing and housing supply. Before moving to the UK, she was involved in educational research and evaluation in Chicago schools. She started her career in the UK in social services policy development in a London local authority and was director of housing and corporate strategy for the Royal Borough of Kensington and Chelsea until moving to the Government Office for London where she was responsible for housing and local government. In 2013, she was recognized by the Queen with the honor of Commander of the British Empire (CBE) for her services to homelessness. Ms. Alafat was educated at Dartmouth College, in New Hampshire, and the University of Chicago.

This is her story.

From an early age, Terrie Alafat knew that public sector work was where she belonged. 'When I was in high school I was always the person organizing to pick up litter, to get rid of drugs or other school activities like that. I didn't know where or how but I did always think I'd be in the public sector. Maybe that's because my father ran a small business and I knew I didn't want to do that,' she recalls. 'I grew up in a rural area. Most of my friends' parents were not working in the corporate sector, so we didn't think about those sorts of jobs. We thought about the law, because we saw the local lawyer, or schools and education because there was a friend's father who was principal of the school. In some respects, the environment I grew up in somewhat defined at an early age those sorts of options,' she notes.

This is one reason why, unlike many of her university classmates, she didn't do the rounds of interviews with Wall Street companies. 'When I graduated from Dartmouth College, I was headed in a different direction. It's fair to say, however, that I didn't think I'd end up in the British Civil Service. Most people thought,' she remembers, 'I'd be a lawyer or in the American Foreign Service given my interests.'

As an undergraduate, Ms. Alafat studied government with an eye to going into law as a route into public service. As is the case for many undergraduates, she found herself interested in a wide variety of subjects. 'I studied Russian and went on two foreign study programs. One was in Leningrad[1] and the other in Romania during the Ceausescu regime. At the time, because I was in one of the early classes with women at Dartmouth,[2] I had a couple of professors, both male, who took me under their wings and mentored me. One of them was Charles McLane, a fantastic guy. I was taking his Soviet politics course and studying Russian; he approached me and said, "I really want you to go on the Romanian program, Terrie." It was unusual to have such a program, especially under the Ceausescu regime. It was a small program, only five of us, and I was the only woman,' she recounts.

During her time in Romania, she worked on a project looking at the Ceausescu regime's approach to the Middle East, which differed from the approach of the Soviet Union. The result of her participation in the program was a shift in Ms. Alafat's course of studies to a much more international focus in comparative government. Her interest in the Middle East was also stirred, as was a desire to study Arabic. Her other mentor at Dartmouth, Gene Garthwaite, a professor in the Middle Eastern Studies Department, encouraged her to go to Cairo. She was awarded the Reynolds Scholarship from Dartmouth, which made it possible to spend a year in Cairo after graduation.

After her year in Cairo, she decided to stay on to improve her Arabic. 'During one of my breaks friends and I traveled to Turkey and traveled down the coast from Istanbul through Syria to Beirut. It was at a time when there was a lull in the fighting in Lebanon so that would have been 1978 or 1979. We went to Beirut and visited

International College, a co-educational preparatory school affiliated with the American University of Beirut. They were restarting their teaching intern program and asked if we were interested. Two of us decided to do it, so that's how I got to Beirut. I started teaching there and then was offered a job while I was applying to graduate school,' she states.

While she was in Beirut, she began work on a masters degree in education. During her second year there, she met her husband. They moved back to the United States and she began doctoral studies in comparative education at the University of Chicago. 'I had reached the conclusion while I was in Cairo and Beirut that I didn't want to do just a straight Foreign Service job. I was still interested in the public sector, but wanted to do something in development, something that would have real impact. I didn't want to push paper. I wanted to be involved in helping developing countries enhance educational systems. I suppose it's still a passion,' she observes, 'given my involvement with Lebanese American University and the Women's Institute. It's fair to say, however, that I didn't think I'd end up an expert in housing in the UK, but here I am over 30 years out of the US with dual citizenship.'

While at the University of Chicago she learned how to do social policy development and research. 'While I was there,' she recalls, 'I was involved in two research projects – one was in the public schools in Chicago and a second was leading a national evaluation program for math curriculum. They were very good training in research and social policy, which has stood me in good stead. The skills apply whether you're working in housing or social services or education.'

While she was working on her dissertation, she and her husband moved to London for his work. Working from a distance was difficult enough, but doing so in a completely new and foreign environment compounded the difficulty. 'After about six months,' Ms. Alafat admits, 'I thought I was going to go crazy. So I took a research job in the Royal Borough of Kensington and Chelsea, a local authority in London.[3] I was definitely overqualified for the job, but what a fun job. I was doing research and learning how things are run in the UK, so that was fantastic. I was given projects which would involve going out to nurseries and older people's housing.'

After a few years she was asked to do policy work as well and quickly rose up the ranks to become responsible for all of the borough's policy development and planning – strategic planning, development planning and planning with the health service. 'Again, it was very interesting,' Ms. Alafat notes, 'because it broadened my responsibilities. At that point I was responsible for a team of about 20 people. Then we restructured; I became a director, which was an interesting period. We were bringing housing and social services together which meant managing a much bigger department. That was a leap to managing a department of about 200 people. What I found fascinating,' she recalls, 'was creating a completely new department with staff from the two departments with their different cultures and backgrounds. We did a lot of work defining what we were all about, what we were trying to achieve, which was quite different from what we had done before. It was actually acknowledging that we needed to do things quite differently.'

The period of consolidation and restructuring resulted in significant achievements including work on mental health and connecting housing services, social services and the health agenda. 'Homelessness – we did a lot of work on homelessness,' she observes.

> That's how I became involved in housing. I came with research and social policy skills and had done research work in social services. Over time the agenda broadened out and with each case the connections were more obvious. That's what's always interested me – and been a driving force – understanding the connections between different things and how there can be a real impact for particular groups of people.

Though still working for Kensington and Chelsea, she began working across London as well. 'Once you get to be in a senior position,' she explains, 'there's a network of senior people from the other boroughs. There was a London-wide housing directors' group that I attended. At that point, only two of us were women. It's still a bit the same in housing which is a male dominated profession. There are exceptions,' she notes:

> if you look at the specialist housing – for aging, disability, homelessness. There you'll see many more women, but looking at housing overall – for example building housing – it's men, almost all men. A fair number of people come into it having been chartered surveyors, engineers, or whatever. As part of that wider group, we did some

interesting things to tackle homelessness across London and I was taking the lead in that.

As a result of her working in housing, she was invited to join the Government Office for London to help develop a London housing strategy. After about a year she became the Director of Homelessness in the British government tasked with developing a strategy and programs to reduce homelessness. She stayed in the civil service and her responsibilities expanded over the years covering various housing policy areas and she became Director of Housing in the Department for Communities and Local Government. She left government in 2015 to take up the position of Chief Executive of the Chartered Institute of Housing, a nonprofit organization, educational charity and professional body which influences policies to improve housing and to ensure all people have access to appropriate and affordable housing in safe and vibrant communities.

'Overall, I'd have to say, it hasn't been a straight path,' she says reflecting on her career. 'The consistent thing is that I've always worked. I've never taken a career break. I've always looked for the next thing that interested me. My husband always says, "There is a lot of consistency in what you've done. You majored in government, you're working in government, and you're working in the public sector." But it's not as if I said that I was going to go into housing. It was more about working in different areas, trying different things, and finding what you enjoy, not worrying too much about skills you learn and don't end up using. I think some young people see it as a much more straight and narrow path, but life really isn't like that,' she asserts.

'It's the opportunities that present themselves,' she continues, 'and whether you choose to take one or not. And they're difficult choices. Obviously completing my Ph.D. went by the wayside when I started working. Though to be fair, once I had my first child I remember my mother-in-law saying, "Now stop working and finish it." I could have done that, but continuing to work was a choice I made. Would I have had a better or more interesting career? Who knows. Will I always regret it a bit? Yes, probably, but it isn't a waste; it's just I've taken a slightly different path. We can probably all think of examples in our lives like that,' she suggests.

'One of the things that has made it much easier for me than it might have been, is a husband who always knew I was going to work and always supported me right through it. I mean right through it. There was never, ever an issue about his career taking dominance over my career,' she insists, 'and never resentment at the time I needed to put into it. I'm not certain every woman or every man has that.'

That sense of partnership and support was evident when children arrived. 'We really both had to pitch in and do what needed to be done and survive the fact that we were both working. Both times, I went back to work nine weeks after the babies were born. That was a choice I made. Living in the UK probably helped to make that choice because I could get a nanny. For a bit, my in-laws were living in London, but for the most part we didn't have family close by and that can be a huge barrier,' Ms. Alafat notes. 'I had a wonderful nanny for seven years, but she was ready to move to other interests, so there was a period when I didn't have reliable childcare and that was a real nightmare. I'd get phone calls and have to manage around it. There's no question that was a challenge. I guess I was fortunate – I remember a friend who worked in investment banking. We used to compare notes and I wondered how she was going to manage. She had to be out at night entertaining clients and had no flexibility. At the time I was working in local government. It's not that I had a nine-to-five job, I didn't,' she recalls. 'But I had a lot of control over my evenings. I knew when I had evening meetings and could make arrangements accordingly. We did have something called flexitime, and even as a more junior manager, I had three weeks of leave in addition to the national holidays. I wouldn't take all my leave so if one of the children got sick I could take the time off. All those sorts of things are challenges but if you have the right support in place – if you have flexi-working and so on – it can work,' she states.

Still, she thinks that work-life balance continues to be a challenge for those with children at home. 'I do work long hours,' she says, 'but it doesn't really matter for me because I don't have children at home anymore and I have a husband who works very long hours as well. But I am aware of the impact on others; I've watched those who work for me, really good workers – and it's not just a female thing, it's a male thing as well – with young children and it's a bit of a challenge for them. It might even mean taking work home. Work-life balance can be challenging and it can be really difficult if you're doing a good amount of the managing and childcare at home, and you're also trying to advance your career. Where do you have time to do those extra things that people look for and judge you on in terms of advancing? That's the reality, really,' she declares. 'It's something we have to watch in our organization – that really good people aren't held back for those sorts of reasons.'

One of the things Ms. Alafat has observed is that women, particularly when pursuing a career and raising a family, are not as good at networking and pushing themselves forward as they might be. 'I look back at my career and I think overall it has gone pretty well for me,' she says. 'I've had interesting jobs and advanced but there are times when I could have gone for something and done just as good a job as the person who got it – that kind of pushing yourself a bit. I think there are a variety of reasons why this doesn't happen. One is because you're always juggling five million things and trying to do a good job at what you're doing at the time. There's also one's personality. When I look back there were times I might have pushed myself a bit more, just had the confidence to say, "I'm going to go for it!" I know people who go for jobs or opportunities constantly. I'm not that kind of person,' she admits. 'There are people who are always looking for the next thing, but I don't think women tend to promote themselves generally, at least the women I see working around me don't do that. They need some encouragement. Maybe it's because we women think being self-promoting isn't as important compared to the things that we're trying to get done at the time,' she adds.

Ms. Alafat was clear that opportunities exist for women who want to serve in government and rise to leadership positions. She noted the efforts being made to mentor women and to provide opportunities for them to network with each other and with women in senior positions at director and deputy director levels. The efforts, which are within departments as well as across government departments, provide a safe environment for women to ask questions and to build networking groups within and across departments. One of the challenges is to design opportunities that are effective and yet not too time consuming.

A civil service women's round table is one of the initiatives designed to meet that challenge. 'It's sort of a speed mentoring session. What it was – and I thought it was a great idea – was inviting young fast streamers and others to come for one hour – because part of the problem is time, just time. Come for one hour.

We had women directors from across government and the participants had five minutes with this person and then five minutes with the next and so on. It was an opportunity for the younger women to ask questions – whatever questions they had on their own mind about their career. Questions varied: "Why did you want to be director?" "Do you think we've got it right in terms of equal opportunities?" It just depended on the person. There was a wide range of questions but it was great, because it wasn't very much time, so senior people could make time to do it. And in between there was a little time for having a cup of tea and networking, which was also very helpful because I realized – I went to it and thought, gosh I haven't seen so and so in a long time. Government is so big,' she points out, 'that unless you're actually doing a project with another department, you don't tend to see people as much.'

Mentoring and having an opportunity for a one-on-one arrangement to talk in a safe space about challenges and difficulties is also important according to Ms. Alafat, who has mentored both women and men working in government as well as in other sectors. 'Sometimes it's about negotiating organizational politics which is difficult regardless of industry sector. In that situation, what's really important is trying to understand where the other person is coming from. You have to try to understand why that other person is doing what they're doing,' she insists.

'The second thing,' she continues, 'is understanding how the organization operates and who makes the decisions, who is influencing who, and who is having what conversations. That's just so important. I learned that early on. I guess the good thing about having moved around in different organizations is that you recognize you really do have to suss out[4] what the organization is all about. It's the same thing moving to other countries; you have to suss out the situation. When I went into the civil service I found it very different to the local authority. In both cases you work for politicians. At the local level, however, the politicians you work for tend to be there for a long time so there's an environment that has some stability. Also, there's an informality and proximity so trust is quickly built. In the civil service, ministers can change every year and there's more formality and less direct day-to-day contact. This can make it more difficult to establish trust which is absolutely key,' she emphasizes. 'I had to figure out how the organization worked.'

A third area to consider is teamwork and recognition. 'In most places I've worked, the best stuff we've done is part of a team effort,' she remarks. 'You have to know how to be part of a team. And the team has to get credit. I guess the difficulty comes if you're never recognized. Then it's really about how you're working with your manager, how you work with other people so that you are valued for what you do. You do get the recognition then. I just don't think the "me, me, me" thing really works that well. I know it works at times. I've seen people do it but I just think it doesn't work in the long run,' she maintains.

From Ms. Alafat's perspective younger women have different attitudes about work. As she noted earlier, when she graduated from university it was assumed women would have full-time careers. 'I think young people now, and women in particular, are not so single minded. They're a little bit more willing to take a career break, to do some other things. My husband tells our two daughters all the time to make certain they can always earn their own living and I think he's right. But I'm not certain everybody sees it like that. It's not because you need to have your own bank accounts,' she claims. 'It's that sense that you can stand on your own two feet and you're going to be able to be independent, to manage, to be able to work one way or another whatever life throws at you. Now that's a very seventies thing,' she admits. 'We always thought we're all going to have our parts to play; we're all going to work. I'm not certain that's the way younger people are thinking now. I think so far my daughters think that way, but I wonder really.'

The other change that she's observed centers on job security and stability in the workplace. The expectation people had of joining an organization and being employed there throughout their careers has shifted not just in the private sector but in the public sector as well. 'People of my generation who entered the civil service thought it was for life,' she says. 'They were entering straight out of university. It was a life, a career and it was a pretty good career because you could be moved around, you had huge opportunity, good development, good pension, not a huge salary but comfortable. It feels less secure now because people are losing their jobs or have lost jobs because of changes; pensions are changing, so the pension is not as good. There's beginning to be a recognition that people might not be spending their whole careers in government, but may need to do things outside government,' she remarks. 'In that context, you have to be thinking about what the next move might be because you're not going to be able to stay comfortably in one spot.'

Ms. Alafat warns against being the kind of person who only aims for the top spot. 'I think that would be quite frustrating because there're not very many top spots and there are lots of good things to do, lots of interesting, challenging jobs. It's important to be thinking about other opportunities and options,' she advises. That said, she does believe there is still a gender imbalance at senior levels that must be addressed in the private sector as well as in government.

'The intake of fast streamers is pretty balanced, but there aren't enough women in senior positions in government. I think it's because of all the reasons I've already indicated. There's probably a need for more tailored support for women,' she adds. 'Some people disagree with me, I know, but I think the reality is that with the resources available and the demands and expectations placed on people it is really hard for them to rise to senior positions. Now that isn't just a female thing, but if we're actually trying to correct the imbalance, I personally think we have to do something extra. It doesn't have to be a lot extra but we need to make certain that people are putting themselves forward,' she argues.

'Resilience is a real factor,' Ms. Alafat remarks, recalling a question she was once asked. 'It was about tips for resilience, how to maintain resilience. What a fascinating question, because it's showing that people are wondering how to cope with the workload and the pressure. We need to attend to it. Whether we think there's a glass ceiling or not, leadership needs to be doing things to make certain that we keep and encourage women to go through the organization so they get to those senior leadership positions. There's a similar discussion taking place about not enough women being recruited in to the boardroom; they're all desperate to get women into the boardroom. But in order to get women into the boardroom,' Ms. Alafat contends, 'you've got to have enough women go through the system.'

'The next generation, our daughters, are entering into a work world that is very different from the one we entered. It's more competitive, certainly. But there are direct efforts being made to support women so that more of them can get through the system and we will have a better balance of women and men in senior leadership positions.'

LEADERSHIP STYLE

Terrie Alafat exemplifies systemic leadership. Working within and across government entities, she demonstrates how to negotiate complex organizations and different cultures. Her tenacity and flexibility coupled with her collaborative approach have enabled her to successfully build partnerships among diverse groups to get the job done.

NOTES

1. Leningrad was the name used from 1924 to 1991 for Saint Petersburg, Russia, known for its history and culture.
2. Dartmouth first admitted women in the fall of 1972; it was the last of the Ivy League schools to do so.
3. Royal Borough of Kensington and Chelsea is one of 14 Inner London boroughs, or municipal units; those boroughs together with 19 Outer London boroughs make up the metropolitan county of Greater London.
4. 'Suss out' is a British phrase meaning to understand or discover something.

14. Claire Jenkins: Non-Executive Director, Sports Direct International plc

Claire Jenkins is a non-executive director of Sports Direct International plc and Media for Development, co-chairman of Amicus and a member of the UK advisory board of Board Apprentice. Her most recent executive role was as Group Director Corporate Affairs, and a member of the executive leadership team, at Rexam plc. Prior to that, Ms. Jenkins was Director, Investor Relations and Group Planning, and a member of the management committee, at Gallaher Group plc. She has held a number of other directorships, including as a non-executive director of Retro Classics Fund, and been a consultant, having started her career as a stockbroker in 1985. Claire holds a degree in theology from the University of St. Andrews.

This is her story.

When she left university, Claire Jenkins had no intention of pursuing a career. 'My original plan had been to work until I got married and had babies,' she says. 'I had no intention of working after I was married. Until that time, I wanted to have a job that (a) paid me really well, because I quite like a nice lifestyle, thank you very much, so given the choice I'll go for a better paid job than a not so well paid job and (b) wanted to be using my brain while I was working. I did not want a "play job," but I still didn't think of myself at all as a career person. Everything was a stepping stone until the other side of my life when I would be married.'

Her degree was in theology which, she notes, 'is not exactly a great degree for going into the City.'[1] She found, however, that it seemed to work in her favor. 'People were so astounded that someone with a theology degree would want to be in the City that it would get me the first interview. It doesn't get you the job,' she observes, 'but pretty much the first question when I was doing the job rounds that last year of university was, "You're doing theology; why do you want to come into the City?" Actually, there's something about standing out, and in the UK the mid-1980s was a great time to be a graduate looking for a job. There were more jobs than there were graduates. I had a choice of jobs offered to me, and I had a pretty rubbish CV at that point.'

In 1985 she began work as a graduate trainee in a brokerage house in the City. She was the first professional woman to work at the firm. 'There was a lot of sexism in the City at that time,' she recalls. 'I remember one time being told by one man, "We think you ought to wear make-up in the office, it's more professional with the clients." My response was, "Well, I'm in charge of the Scottish desk, so how can they tell I'm wearing make-up down the telephone when I'm in London?" There was a pause after which he came out with, "Well, it would be much nicer for all of us." What's fascinating to me, when I look back on it,' she continues, 'was the sexism was not from the 50 and 60 year olds, the sexism was from people my age and a bit older. What actually happened was that a lot of the 50 and 60 year olds who had never worked with women apart from support staff said to me quite early on, "I just want you to know that if I ever do or say something that offends you, would you please tell me; you know this is new to me but I want it to work." And one of them, when I looked a bit quizzical, said, "My daughter is about to leave university and I want her to have opportunities. I realize the world is a different place now." I thought about it afterwards. Very shortly after I joined another girl also joined as a graduate trainee. For us, the older men were not only the ones who had given us the jobs – it wasn't that they were being patronizing and it wasn't that they made allowances – but also they did think of us as being trailblazers for their children. Our own generation of men and the ones who were in their thirties resented us fearfully, however, because, of course, we increased the competition. The problems I encountered in the City, I encountered from people five to ten years older than me, not from the old guard.'

In the early 1990s the UK was dealing with a recession and many were losing their jobs. Ms. Jenkins was among them. Rather than being despondent, she saw the situation as an opportunity. 'I learned a lot in those seven plus years, but I was ready to leave. I didn't want to be beholden to a boss again, so, I decided to do my own stuff,' she says.

She began to do consulting work. 'I had been selling equities to fund managers,' she explains, 'so thought maybe I could do a spot of light marketing to start with, as I imagined there were some transferable skills. The first thing I did was act as an agent for an artist. What I knew about modern art could be written on the back of a postage stamp. I literally was on the phone to journalists before his exhibition thumbing through the Thames & Hudson guide to impressionism saying, "His work is very like, uh – Monet." I didn't even know the names of the artists. I'd never done a press release before, so I looked up "press releases" and saw there was a rough structure to them and thought, "well, I'll give that a go." This sounds awfully conceited, but I thought how difficult can it be? Marketing is promoting, getting people interested and so forth. That all said, I should like to add that my time at Gallaher did teach me that there is, in reality, a lot more to excellent marketing and brand building than I had realized at the time!'

She expanded her client base to include a catering company and a restaurant. 'The restaurant was doing very well at dinner but not doing very well at lunch. I decided that we should go around to local businesses and make them lunch members and give them special benefits, so I developed something called a lunch club. It was, in effect, a loyalty card scheme. This was long before Starbucks and its loyalty card,' she notes.

Given her knowledge of the City and her contacts, Ms. Jenkins also began doing investor relations; after a while it was taking up most of her time. Eventually, she and a colleague, who worked on some projects with her, ended up founding a company. The business was successful. 'We got big enough that we needed to have an office, and employees, so,' she adds, 'I ended up being back in an office as opposed to working from home. The company was in investor relations, which in the mid-1990s was very much an infant profession.' After a time, she realized her attitude was changing. As she puts it, 'I wanted to get close to one company – to be "doing" and taking responsibility for my views as opposed to advising a selection of companies. So, in 1997 I joined Gallaher, the international tobacco company.'[2]

She joined Gallaher as a senior manager. It was a move that changed her perspective on work. Joining Gallaher 'was a revelation; it was the most marvelous place to work. It was extraordinary – an incredibly nurturing, amazing environment where you were just stretched way beyond where you thought you could be,' she declares. 'My line about Gallaher is that your boss gave you something new to do six months before you realized you were bored; and they moved people around – somebody who'd been in distribution got moved to be head of HR; somebody who'd been in UK commercial got made head of corporate affairs. You were not kept in a box and therefore, if you were somebody who found things interesting outside your direct remit, it was like "ship it in, ship it in." It was fabulous,' she continues, enthusiastically. 'It also just happened to be an incredibly fun place to work; the people were just wonderful, so it was not at all difficult to absolutely want to be focused and driven, and my career just accelerated within sort of nanoseconds. By 2000 I was put on the ExCo.[3] At the time, I was 37 years old, so extraordinary. And there's a huge amount of luck. I'm afraid I do believe that in life there is so much that you can do for yourself – you know it's all about broadening your experiences, accepting challenges, the sort of person you are and can make yourself be – but I have to say, there's an element of luck too. Being in the right place at the right time to grab opportunities is luck,' she contends.

From her perspective, this is exactly what happened with the Gallaher position. 'At the end of 1996, when I had decided I wanted to go in-house and therefore was open to calls from headhunters,' she recounts, 'I was getting a lot of calls from headhunters. Investor relations was in its infancy. I was one of the literally about ten people in the UK market at that time who could legitimately call themselves an investor relations professional. Although more companies wanted to create the role in-house there were a limited number of people they could call. It wasn't going to be a case of it taking me months to find something. If the Gallaher job had been three months later, I'd have already been somewhere else. There is luck; and I'm afraid sometimes people are lucky – and on this occasion I was – and sometimes they're not and that's a sad fact of life,' she observes.

She remained at Gallaher for ten years until it was taken over in 2007. The takeover was not a surprise. 'To be honest,' she says, 'we always knew it was going to happen. We were the largest of the second-tier tobacco companies and tobacco is a consolidating industry. Whenever the time came we just had to make sure we got the best possible price and that we looked after the majority of our people. But we always knew that senior management would all go. So that happened. I then – to be honest – took a bit of time out, which was rather lovely,' she adds.

Her plan was to take a year off and do a lot of traveling. 'I had this bright idea,' she recalls, 'that between trips I would have the odd coffee with headhunters so as to line something up, and that I would start a new position in the first quarter of 2009. Then there was a bit of an oops, a spot of a financial crisis. But the other thing about me is that I'm a Pollyanna. I'm very much of the view that things will always work out and if it takes a bit longer, it takes a bit longer. I was not going to slit my wrists over it.'

From the beginning, she was clear that she would still do some consulting even while traveling. 'I wanted to keep my hand in so I didn't look like a complete lazy cow,' she says. 'Again, there was an element of luck. One of my main clients,' she states, 'was a company called Sports Direct. They were looking for communications, investor relations and corporate governance advice. I absolutely adored them; they reminded me of the Gallaher personalities, and I worked really well with them. That carried on for a while, though not full time; in 2008 and into 2009 I was consulting with them and doing a few other bits and bobs.'

By this point, Ms. Jenkins was much more focused on her career. Her plan was to be a full-time executive until her mid-50s and then to develop a non-executive director portfolio, or move 'plural' as she puts it. In 2010, she was offered and accepted a full-time position at Rexam.[4] 'Again this was incredibly lucky,' she notes, 'because it was in corporate affairs, an area that I didn't have on my CV, an area that I'd been trying to break into.' She was considered an expert in investor relations (IR) and strategic planning because of her responsibilities at Gallaher; this was not the case with corporate affairs since she did not have direct responsibility for that area.

She explains the dilemma: 'I was the only communicator on the ExCo at Gallaher; the corporate affairs fellow wasn't on the ExCo, which meant that I represented corporate affairs at that level even though the department didn't report to me. I was trying to look for positions with a similar broad role at the ExCo level but I was having a real problem because Gallaher was about the only company that ever put IR on the ExCo. In most companies, corporate affairs is on ExCo and IR isn't. At Gallaher, it had been the other way around. We'd been the other way around because that was the way Gallaher was run. They didn't put things into boxes so there wasn't a sort of "Let's take a management template off a bookshelf" approach. So, I was having a bit of a problem because the only way for me to have the level of job I wanted was to be in corporate affairs, but I was having people come back to me saying, "But you've never been line responsible." What was amazing was Rexam offered me corporate affairs without IR in the position, which meant that I was actually going to be able to demonstrate that I wasn't going to rest on my laurels of IR. I was going to be able to demonstrate that I could take corporate affairs on despite my "official record." That was great,' she concludes.

She was at Rexam for just under three years; she left for a combination of reasons. 'One of the main ones,' she says, 'was that I'd done everything that had to be done – revitalizing the communications function and instigating, developing and rolling out a company-wide sustainability strategy. In addition, the company had halved during that period because we'd done lots of selling off of divisions. Rexam just didn't need somebody at my level any longer.'

But her time at Rexam is only part of the story. 'What also happened,' she recalls, 'which was rather nice, was when I'd gone in-house at Rexam, and had to tell my clients goodbye, Sports Direct were actually a bit upset. They asked if I couldn't still consult. I reminded them that I'd told them all along that I was looking for the right full-time executive role and that when I found it I would cease consulting. Anyway, they came back to me and offered me a non-executive director position. They really wanted my input. When I first began consulting for them my dealings were primarily with the CEO; by the time I told them I was leaving to go in-house at Rexam I was giving advice to the board on corporate governance issues, remuneration issues, and other issues, as well as the original areas; I was effectively doing things that non-executive directors do. They told me they'd had a chat and thought I was a natural fit. I understood their business and I'd be a very valuable non-exec director. They also said one of the things they liked about me was that I have no problem expressing views, including expressing contrary views. I tend to do that tactfully and politely. I use humor a lot. So, I'll make my point, but I'll do it in such a way that people are smiling while I'm making it. I think they appreciated that; I would sometimes say quite critical things but I would say them in a non-aggressive way.'

For Ms. Jenkins, this was, 'of course, again a bit of luck.' She is adamant. 'The hardest non-exec position to get is your first,' she says and quickly adds, 'of course, it took everything in my control not to jump up and down and hug them when they offered this to me. There I was at 47 being offered a non-exec directorship, which would see me through to when I wanted to go plural, and I'd have a plc under my belt.[5] The luck element here,' she posits, 'is that I'm not sure any other plc would have done what they did because it's not the normal route.'

Asked about the future for women in leadership positions, Ms. Jenkins identified a number of things that can hold women back or are differences between men and women in the workplace. 'One thing that I think is a difference between men and women is something often said anecdotally but I think there's truth to it: Women will be honest about what they can do, whereas men will "wing it" a bit more.' She explains, 'Women in interviews tend to be more honest than men about what their achievements are. A woman in an interview for a job might say, "I was part of a team, I played a major role in the team, but it couldn't have happened without my colleagues." Whereas, it's quite possible that a man will say, "I did this; I did that." That's been said anecdotally, every article I've ever read says it, and it is, to an extent, my experience as well. Maybe because I am a woman and I'm like that myself, I don't like "I, I, I." There's no "I" in "TEAM." Most things that you achieve,' she insists, 'you achieve not just because of your own hard work, focus and drive; but it's because of the team around you or the resources you've been able to call upon. People who don't recognize that are a real pain to work with.'

She also believes that there's a tendency among some women not to try new things or take on projects in areas that are outside of their responsibilities because they lack expertise. 'They'll hold back,' she says, 'even if they are very talented individuals; they won't volunteer and they might even say no when asked. Whereas, I think equally bright and ambitious men will never do that. I think one of the reasons that I've been successful – alongside that I absolutely have a thing about acknowledging the team or whoever else has helped me – is that whenever it's been something I've never done before, my attitude has always been, "What the hell, let's give it a go." I actively enjoy the "pit-in-the-tummy" feeling, that sense of "how am I going to do this?" This is certainly how it was when I left the City and started to do consulting,' she acknowledges.

When she joined Gallaher, she found a conducive environment for this approach. 'Gallaher was marvelous,' she says. 'Whenever the question was, "Does anyone have any thoughts about how we can tackle X?" I would stick my hand up and say, "Well, I'll give it a go."' As an example, she described changes made to the annual two-day strategic away meeting of Gallaher's board. The focus of the meeting was to update non-executive directors on industry issues, company issues and strategic issues and to provide time for the full board to explore strategic options. 'In tobacco,' Ms. Jenkins notes, 'a lot of it had to do with mergers and acquisitions and the "Big Six." The meetings were pretty boring, the same sort of interminable PowerPoint presentations and such that most corporates use. One year the chief executive said he wanted to achieve two things at the strategy meeting: make it more interesting and enlivening, and to start exposing more and more management to the board.'

From her perspective, this is a sign of a very well-managed company. 'A lot of companies,' she explains, 'keep people who are below board level away from the board, whereas the Gallaher CEO's view was different. He wanted the board to see the depth of management. The first time he did it, he came to my office in February and said, "I want you to design a day and I want these five people to be exposed to the board and I want it to be done in such a way that it's really fun. Can you do it?" It was nothing to do with investor relations or strategic planning. He did ask if I had the time, so it would have been very easy for me to say no.'

Of course, she accepted the challenge and responded in a very creative way. 'I asked each of the five regional heads to pretend to be the chief exec of one of our five major competitors and to give a presentation on how the competitors were going to undo Gallaher. It also had an added bonus because the five heads of regions had to work together on all the presentations so they grew closer too. So, the head of Russia had to tell the others what each of them as "competitors" were doing in Russia and so on. This exercise broadened everyone's knowledge. It achieved so many things in terms of improving the meeting. It was very successful and the board loved it. Of course, unfortunately, that sort of landed me with it, because each year after that it was, "What are you going to do that's different?" It was a great challenge, but it was fun. Though it was completely not part of my job description, the idea of saying "no" to the CEO just didn't cross my mind,' she concludes.

From her perspective saying yes to challenges is an important element in being successful. 'I think it's probably one of the major differences when you talk about people being weeded out as they go up the pyramid. In most organizations the people who go up the pyramid are the people who never say no to a new challenge,' she states. She thinks the next generation of women has to accept the need to get out of their comfort zone. As she puts it, 'they need to aim for the pit-in-the-tummy.'

She was never part of a formal mentoring program, but had a number of informal mentors, all of whom were men. She insists, 'there was no way my career would have developed if I hadn't had somebody on occasion to go to and say, "I'm not sure how to cope with this" or "this is going on" or whatever – not the practical stuff but more the social networks and the personalities and things like that. There was also an element of practicality involved. I wanted to know what skills I needed to develop in order to be promoted. It's the kind of question you can ask a mentor if you can't ask your direct boss. So, yes,' she says, 'I think it's important to mentor young women, but I also think, as a senior woman, it's equally as important to be mentoring talented young men, and I think that senior men should be mentoring both genders too.'

If for some reason there aren't mentors or people in the office who are supportive, she advises developing a network outside of the office. 'Nobody needs to be completely isolated,' she insists. 'You can always find a network. It can be alumni from university. It can be school friends. It can be mentoring outfits. Everybody can find somebody if they haven't got it in their own organization. If you're lucky enough, you'll have it in the organization and you won't need to find it elsewhere. But if you haven't got it, then go and make a bit of an effort to get it.'

She is clear that every job has an element of administrative efficiency to it, has a 'to do' list, has particular goals and objectives. The task is to be clear about the objectives and to identify the three or four things that will make it possible to achieve the objectives. 'It doesn't matter whether you're a housekeeper or chief executive of Apple,' she says. 'If you always make sure that you cover all your objectives, whatever it is you're doing, if you say to yourself, "I need to do x, x and x to achieve y," then you can do the building blocks. If you look at it the other way around and start with the big picture, it can be overwhelming.'

Asked about the push by some in the European Union to establish quotas for female representation on company boards, Ms. Jenkins is clear that she does not favor the quota system. 'I don't agree with quotas. They can lead to the appointment of women who are neither qualified nor particularly talented. I don't think that helps women's causes,' she maintains. 'The fundamental problem, I think, with UK boards is that we've moved to the US model of only having two executive directors on the board, the chief executive and the finance director, with all the remaining executives being below board level. That's the reason there's a shortage of talent for non-exec director positions because those execs are not gaining any board experience. Gallaher had five executives on the board of directors and six or sometimes seven non-execs. It still met the combined code about the majority of board members being non-exec, but two things happened. You had people gaining valuable board experience, and, from my perspective, you had an organization that was actually better run because you have more collective responsibility, cabinet responsibility. For example,' she continues, 'the other executive directors are actually getting involved in capital structure issues, which they don't get involved in when all they're doing is heading a division. They're getting exposed to which issues really matter to the non-exec directors and shareholders, and they're also more united with the chief exec and the finance director, which means there's less bickering. I think it's a crying shame that the UK has moved to the American model. That also reduces the number of women in the pool because you would have more women as executive directors if you've got more posts of executive directors which in turn means there'd be more women eligible for non-exec board positions.'

From Ms. Jenkins' perspective, advancing to the board level and receiving that first non-executive director appointment is not just difficult for women. It is difficult for men as well. She points to the process often used to fill those positions. 'Most board chairs and most nominating committees are really, really boring and try to play safe,' she states. 'The brief they will give the headhunter is that previous plc board experience is necessary. How are you supposed to get experience if you don't get a first appointment?' she asks. One change she recognizes is the push for diversity in the boardroom. 'More women from ExCos are getting on boards,' she reports.

Another change that she has seen is a move toward a female style of management and leadership. 'Even in organizations that have not made it yet to the new way of doing things,' she observes, 'there is an understanding and acceptance that the world has changed and that leadership has got to be much more consensual and collaborative and to be about inspiring and team building and so on rather than just barking orders at people.' Ms. Jenkins believes women are more inclined toward this style of management. 'Generally speaking we don't like overt conflict, even when there are disagreements across the table. When people have different opinions, what successful women do is find a way to get to a common ground having let everybody have a say and then if there isn't consensus saying, "Well, the table's split down the middle; here's my decision. I know that's going to disappoint some of you; if I'm wrong, I'm wrong, but I'm paid to make a decision." It needs to be done in a way to never humiliate somebody in terms of losing an argument,' she stresses. 'I think women are just naturally much better at that and I think the world is moving more in that direction which works in the favor of women coming up the ranks,' she states. Her advice to other women is, 'if that side of your management style isn't recognized and accoladed or validated, don't change your style, change the company because the vast majority of workplaces are recognizing that the collaborative approach is more successful in the long run.'

Another piece of advice she has for women is very direct. 'Don't try and be a man,' she says. 'There are exceptions to every rule, but my general experience with women is that we actually are better prepared to express a contrary opinion once we've gone beyond a hurdle of nervousness, which I think in the long run is really good.

If you don't take a stand and speak up, you lose something that when you get towards the top of your career makes you stand out. Early in your career it doesn't really come up. Middle of your career it comes up and there's a risk that you could alienate people and get yourself sidelined, which can be a problem since it's toward the end of your career that I think it's so valuable and makes you stand out,' she asserts.

She credits her family and her education for her strong sense of self-confidence. 'Two things were massive influences,' she says. 'It was absolutely wonderful being a mistake born eight years later because you don't just have your parents, you have the elder siblings who think you're marvelous, wonderful, and the fact that you can say the word "hello" means you're Einstein; so, my self-confidence was amazing, courtesy of that. The other thing is that my mother is a bright woman who never had a chance to use her brain fully. She was born in 1923, in a completely different era. She got sent to a very nice Catholic school in Edinburgh where they were taught how to manage the housekeeper and whatever. She never sat an examination. It was a ridiculous education and she always resented it. She was always determined that if she had daughters, they would have equal opportunities. And my father was really happy with that. They chose Roedean, which was not a smart grand school but one where you learn that you can do whatever you want to do. If what you want is to get married and have babies, that's fine. If what you want to do is be a typist, that's fine. And if you want to be a nuclear scientist, that's also fine. Roedean was amazing. As long as whatever you wanted to do was your choice and not someone else's choice for you, it was validated.'

While self-confidence has clearly contributed to her success, Ms. Jenkins indicates that her ability to work well with people is the key to her career. 'You are never going to be successful in your career if you're not able to work well within teams – if you're not able to pull people together and get them all going in the same direction. You'll be fine without that skill at a lower level, and there may be jobs where you can be a loner, but in corporate life you need to be able to get on with others and with those junior to you and those higher up,' she insists.

'The nicest thing in the whole of my time at Rexam and there was an awful lot that I achieved there, the thing that made me the happiest,' she declares 'was that in the employee engagement survey I got an engagement score of 92 on a personal level for leadership together with the Company Secretary – our functions were merged for the survey. That was the highest of anybody on the ExCo where the average was 69. That's what my career is now. Fifteen or 20 years ago,' she notes, 'my career was about the practical, about whether I could write an investor presentation or some such. My career now is focused on leadership and team building; can I get a team, small or large – whatever it is they need to be doing – to go in the same direction and to enjoy doing it while they're doing it?'

LEADERSHIP STYLE

Claire Jenkins is an extraordinarily complex leader. What we learn most importantly from her is 'never say no.' Do not turn down an opportunity. One of the strengths of Ms. Jenkins is her ability to try almost any position, and then figure out how to make it work. She is a flexible and adaptable leader; two qualities important in leading the global political economies all organizations are part of today. She is also fearless and an extraordinary risk-taker.

NOTES

1. The 'City' refers to the City of London, which is part of Greater London; it is London's financial district.
2. Gallaher Group plc was the world's fifth largest tobacco company when Japan Tobacco bought it in 2007; see http://www.jti.com/about-jti/jti-glance/where-we-operate/europe/united-kingdom/english/overview/.
3. ExCo, or Executive Committee, is a company's management committee comprised of select members of senior management.
4. Rexam plc, a UK-based leading global beverage can maker, was acquired by US-based Ball Corporation in June 2016. See http://phx.corporate-ir.net/phoenix.zhtml?c=115234&p=irol-newsArticle&ID=2181315.
5. 'Plc' stands for 'public limited company' and refers to a company with limited liability that offers shares to the public; it is used primarily in the UK and Ireland and some Commonwealth countries.

15. Francesca Raleigh O'Connell: Founder, SculptureLondon

Francesca Raleigh O'Connell worked in UK institutional stockbroking and corporate advisory for 27 years and is an award-winning equities investment analyst. She has a degree in English Literature and started her career at stockbroker Laing & Cruickshank in 1985. She became a Director of Panmure Gordon at the age of 30 and went on to become a Director at Investec Securities and Numis Securities. She retired in 2012 to pursue new and more varied projects. Her non-executive directorships have ranged from being on the Supervisory Board of Network Rail to being on the Advisory Board of start-up Linkup Battersea, which encourages professional women back into the workplace through volunteer projects for charities. She is also the founder of web portal SculptureLondon.

This is her story.

From the beginning, Francesca Raleigh O'Connell was encouraged to pursue a career. 'My parents felt strongly that I should use my education to get a professional job. We lived in South East Asia so they sent me to Cheltenham Ladies College (CLC), an academic girls-only boarding school in England that reinforced their idea that a woman should be well educated and that women should and could be professionals. Indeed,' she recalls, 'CLC engendered in us that women could achieve anything and even become Prime Minister!' She notes that not all women starting out when she did had that combination of family and educational support. 'In my early months at work I saw some women around me who had great potential but didn't have their hearts in their jobs as they were expecting, or were expected, to give up their full-time jobs when they got married to raise a family,' she says, 'but I was encouraged to do more.'

Ms. Raleigh began her career in the financial services sector in 1985, around the time of Big Bang,[1] when she joined the brokerage firm of Laing & Cruickshank. At the time, there were very few women in the industry. 'I was lucky,' she remarks, 'because the first boss I worked for, Henry Poole, was a great mentor. It was very much a man's world but he was not chauvinistic. He was focused on getting the job done and consequently gave me lots of opportunities. When I started, I did a stint on the Stock Exchange floor, as Henry wanted me to be able to transact client orders if he wasn't around. It was before online trading and a very macho environment. I was a "blue button" – the lowest of the low and given all the grunt work. There were a number of us – a few girls and a lot of boys. The boys on the floor had a harsh rite of passage as the men could be mean to them, but they had a soft spot for us girls.' She laughs as she remembers. 'They once sent me off on a wild goose chase around the trading floor to collect the prices on a stock called *Underseas Airways*. All the men were in on the joke. I was terrified of disappointing my scary Head of Dealing, "The Governor," and was getting increasingly frantic, as the stock didn't appear to exist. After ten minutes I realized that the joke was on me as all the men in the stock exchange were grinning at me!'

It was a very male environment. 'There was a lot of drinking, banter, swearing, dirty jokes, sexist remarks. You had to be thick-skinned, but at the same time you had to have a sense of humor and be fun and be able to mix socially with the guys to move forward. As a girl in that world, you had to choose how you were going to handle yourself. There were a few girls who "played around," but I felt it was important not to do anything in the office that I would regret or that would lose the respect of the men,' she says. 'I worked very hard and made sure when I did anything that I was doing it at least as well as the boys, if not better. I made it my business to learn everything I could and to be very good at what I did.'

She was fortunate in that respect. 'Henry, who recruited and trained me, had very high standards. He was one of the first analysts in the City[2] to do cash flow forecasts and was intellectually rigorous so you had to argue your case thoroughly and convincingly. He was also extremely good on the commercial side, making money for our institutional clients and bringing in the corporate clients and the corporate deals. I learned a lot from him which was important,' she emphasizes, 'because it was a competitive environment where you were only as good as the next deal you were bringing in.'

Once she completed her initial training, Ms. Raleigh moved into the research department as an assistant equities investment analyst, working alongside Henry on the Paper, Packaging, Printing and Publishing sectors where he was the number one rated analyst in the UK Stock Market. She explains the significance of this for her career. 'On the research side, firms prized having high profile number one rated analysts because that meant more business for the firm. Henry taught me my trade well – he was bold, ambitious and innovative, yet had attention to detail and was hard working. He constantly stretched himself and me, giving me a lot of responsibility from a young age. He was however rather eccentric and temperamental but that stood me in good stead to be able to handle the larger-than-life characters I came across later in my career. I went on to practice all he taught me at the future firms I went to. I was always headhunted to come in and build the market-leading position in my sector,' Francesca states.

She had been at Laing & Cruickshank for about eight years when she was headhunted to Panmure Gordon, another London firm, where she became the number one rated analyst in her sectors, overtaking Henry in the ratings, and was made a director at the age of 30. 'I worked at four firms in my career,' she remarks, 'but was always at medium-sized firms. I was offered the chance to go to larger firms, but I didn't take them. I preferred the medium-sized firms because you could be more involved, you knew everybody and everyone knew you. Of course, with all the consolidation in the industry, the medium-sized firms often got taken over and then I'd be at a bigger, more global firm for a bit which was not so much fun,' she observes.

When asked about work-life balance in the investment industry, Ms. Raleigh acknowledged that the quality of life was probably better in a medium-sized firm. 'However, you still had to work hard, if not harder to get the rankings, and the trades as you didn't have a global brand and marketing machine behind you,' she explains. 'It was a very commercial environment,' she continues, 'and once you made Director the measure of success was the ratings you had, the business that you brought in and the deals that came in as a result of your work. This didn't happen easily. You had to work hard and I was that type of person. I was driven to succeed,' she says, 'I loved targets and I loved my work!'

Asked whether women faced challenges that male colleagues did not face Ms. Raleigh indicates that women had to find their own corner but acknowledges that there were times when a different approach to winning business, managing an account or getting a deal done set a tone which appealed to clients. 'However,' she states, 'there were times when you needed to be very firm. Annually, when salaries were being set and bonuses awarded, I went into the meeting with a list of everything I had achieved in that financial year because I felt there was a tendency or leaning toward paying women less if they could get away with it. It became a joke in the firm that my Head of Research would be nervous ahead of our meetings! I was not willing to be paid less than the person next to me when I knew I'd achieved more. It helped to be in an industry that has clear measures of success – ratings and awards as an analyst, market share in trading and winning corporate clients – and I was good at achieving them. That gave me the confidence to fight for what I deserved,' she admits and adds, 'I've always believed in a meritocracy, partly because of my background and what my parents had achieved. If someone has worked hard and delivered on something they should be rewarded for it regardless of age or gender.' She reflects, 'I had to be much more aggressive then than I would now as it was the only way to make your point in those days. The guys had to see that you meant business and couldn't be sidelined.'

Her sense of self-confidence was in part due to the education she received. However, when she and others from her schooldays get together, they agree that one thing was missing. 'While the school was amazing in encouraging us that we could go out and be Prime Minister, it didn't quite explain to us how that ran alongside being a wife and a mother. We've all had to learn that side,' she notes. In the financial services sector at that time there were few older women around to be role models.

When she began her career, most of the women her age were not married. 'In part, that's because the hours were long in the financial sector. Also, there was lots of corporate entertainment with our corporate and investor clients, marketing trips and company site visits. I found that I was working on weekends as well, because I always wanted to be well prepared for the week ahead. So, I probably did more work than I needed to,' she surmises. When she married at 29, she decided to make a few changes. 'I began to draw the line on entertaining late and on doing too much travel,' she says, 'though I would still be going in early and doing work at weekends. Even on holiday, I'd do a bit of work; there would be a project or something that would be on my mind and so I'd work on it.' She feels this was a combination of the pressure from the industry given that large sums of money were at stake, her tendency toward perfection and her desire for achievement.

One of the positive outcomes of all the hard work was achieving financial independence. 'I was lucky not to be the only breadwinner for my family as my husband has a successful career as well. I was highly paid and consequently was financially independent. It was important, for me, to have my own nest egg and not take advantage of him. Also,' she continues, 'the financial independence helped me do my best work and feel free in a corporate environment. I think it will be harder for those following me to have the same feeling of financial independence, especially after the 2008 recession when remuneration packages have been cut.'

Younger women who want to go into financial services will find that the sector is still a political environment, though there have been behavior improvements. 'Irritating sexist behaviors are not tolerated any more. Men have daughters who want to have careers, so they have shaped up. They now realize that the women in their firm could be their daughters, sisters, girlfriends or wives,' she notes.

Her advice to young women is to recognize they need to be multi-skilled. 'The days are gone when you could be a specialist and focus on one area. There's much more expected of you now. You need to be able to pitch for the business, to handhold the corporate and investor clients when issues arise, and to understand the nuts and bolts of what you are doing. When I first started you could be a brilliant sales person or brilliant at finding undervalued stocks or whatever. Now you have to stretch your skills to grasp the whole business, to become a jack-of-all-trades and a master of more than one,' she states.

'Leadership styles have changed as well,' she notes. 'When I first started in the City everything was run by men, many of them were Wykehamists.[3] They were very clever and were in senior positions in the City, in law and other professions. They were old school, had standards and behaved professionally. Then the style of leadership changed to a new breed, often the person who had been the biggest rainmaker.[4] They were not necessarily good leaders. Some abused their positions and there were many *The Wolf of Wall Street*[5] types. Now the leadership is better and calmed down,' she says.

Another change Ms. Raleigh has witnessed is in the boardroom. She saw this through the boards of her corporate clients, the boards of the firms she worked for, as well as in her more recent non-executive directorship roles. 'Boards have become better balanced because of the presence of women,' she contends. 'The dynamics are improved. In an all male boardroom there can be too much testosterone – a desire to take short cuts, hog the conversation, leverage up, to merge with another firm or do a massive acquisition. Women's presence can bring a more measured and considered approach in exploring a process, the merits of transactions, an openness to the potential risks and whether or not they are necessary.' She adds, 'Having said that, women can also make business and strategic mistakes. I did work with a listed company with an aggressive female CEO and CFO which fell into all the testosterone traps!'

Another thing that Ms. Raleigh has noticed is that the proportional increase in women has been more at the non-executive level than the executive level. 'The pool of qualified executive women is still small for what is a large number of non-executive positions,' she says. 'There are still many, many more men in executive positions as CEOs, CFOs and as division heads in firms. The service industry generally is doing better than other industries in terms of the number of women in executive positions, still it seems in the UK to get to senior positions a woman still has to be better than a man. To really change, more women need to become executives, which can be difficult, and women in executive positions don't always help each other.'

'For my generation in the financial services industry it was lonely as a woman in a senior position, as most women didn't last the distance. Even today. We need more women in executive positions in finance. Also, it's important that women hear "You can do it" and that men not be threatened by women in leadership, which I do think is getting better. I think each generation makes it a little easier for those who follow, so I'm very positive that women can succeed,' she declares.

In 2012, Francesca retired from the financial services industry. While being a saver rather than a spender had made it financially possible to do so, there were other reasons as well. 'My son was eight. I wouldn't see him in the morning because I had to be at my desk by seven. When I came home in the evening he was already falling asleep, so I only really saw him at weekends. I think, too, a person's physical appearance shows when they're in a good place, enjoying life, and happy and I was looking at myself in the mirror and a pale person was looking back at me,' she admits. 'I was young to retire – just 48 – but thought others in my age group looked pale and stale as well. Moreover,' she adds, 'to personally progress in this business one had to become a department head or move into corporate finance. I didn't enjoy management as I enjoyed contact with clients and doing original work myself. Also, the people who make money for their firms in the financial sector are rarely the best managers as we're too competitive! The other career avenue for me would have been corporate finance, putting together IPOs and other deals in my sectors; it would have been interesting, but it requires evenings with clients, travel and all of that. I would have been away from home even more, so I rejected that choice.'

It was time to leave, but as an equity partner it needed to be a planned exit. 'One of the jokes in the financial community,' she says good-naturedly, 'is that the only good leaver is a dead leaver! If you are successful at your existing firm they are terrified that you might pop up again at the competition or a start-up and that you'll take your corporate and investor clients with you.' She arranged an orderly departure over a six-month period during which she handed over her projects and clients to others.

'It was a difficult transition after 27 years,' she reports. 'It was very much a lifestyle change. My measure of my worth had been the industry's measures of success. I had to put these aside and figure out new measures of my worth as a person.' Since leaving the financial services industry, Ms. Raleigh has had various non-executive director board positions. She explains, 'This was an eye opener and a privilege. Network Rail had £6bn revenues, about 35,000 employees, invested over £30bn of the UK taxpayers' money every five years in UK infrastructure, and had an unconventional and unique shareholder structure. The supervisory board that I sat on was doing a great job ticking the boxes on professional, gender, ethnic, regional and age diversity, though these were characteristics which were yet to filter through the organization as a whole. At the other end of the spectrum I sit on a predominantly female advisory board and organization, and it has been valuable having two guys on the board with us.'

She has recently founded SculptureLondon,[6] a web portal. 'It's a go-to source to find out about London's sculpture events, collections, rich history and much more,' she says. 'Unlike the financial services sector where it was constant movement to the next thing, the next deal, now I have to be patient about building something. It's keeping my mind stimulated; actually, I think it's keeping my mind more stimulated than it was in the last three or four years of my executive life. I find I like creating something, doing something on my own but also dipping in and out of working with other people. It will be interesting to see how it will develop,' she speculates. 'But hey, my parents always told me I could do anything if I set my mind to it!'

LEADERSHIP STYLE

Francesca Raleigh O'Connell is a flexible leader who fights for her rights and for fairness in the workplace. She demonstrates how one can use one's expertise to leverage a career in many firms. This ability to successfully change jobs and change the direction of one's career is an important trait in contemporary life. Again, like other women leaders, Ms. Raleigh is a fearless advocate of herself and her contributions.

NOTES

1. 'Big Bang' refers to the 1986 deregulation of the financial services industry in the UK. More information is available at http://financial-dictionary.thefree dictionary.com/Financial+Services+Act+1986.
2. The 'City' refers to the City of London, which is part of Greater London; it is London's financial district.
3. Wykehamists are alumni of Winchester College, which was founded in the fourteenth century by William of Wykeham, Bishop of Winchester.
4. Rainmaker refers to a person who brings in business for a firm or organization.
5. *The Wolf of Wall Street* is the title of Jordan Belfort's autobiography which details his rise as a Wall Street stockbroker and the lavish lifestyle that accompanied it and his eventual fall when he was sentenced to a four-year prison term for securities fraud and money laundering. A movie of the same name was produced in 2013.

6. More information on SculptureLondon is available at http://www.sculpturelondon.com.

16. Professor Catherine Peckham, CBE, MD, FMedSci: Professor of Paediatric Epidemiology, University College London

Catherine Peckham is particularly known for her work on infections in pregnancy. She has contributed across a broad range of subjects including infectious disease epidemiology, vaccination policy and the social and biological determinants of health in childhood. The common theme of her work is the impact of infections and other external factors on children's health and the adult consequences of ill health in childhood. She was a founder fellow of the Academy of Medical Sciences and made an honorary fellow of the Royal College of Pathologists and the Royal College of Obstetrics and Gynaecology. In recognition of her services to medicine she was made Commander of the British Empire (CBE). She received the James Spence Medal from the Royal College of Paediatricians and Child Health for her contributions to paediatrics, the Harding Award for the prevention of childhood disability and the Terrence Higgins Trust award for her contribution to HIV in women and children. Her activities have extended outside the sphere of medicine as non-executive director of the Advertising Standards Authority, a UK-US Fulbright Commissioner and Governor of St. Paul's School in London.

This is her story.

'Early in my career I left London and worked as a doctor in a rural community.' This, she says, gave her first-hand experience of the problems of health in a population and pointed her in the direction of her future career. Returning to London after two years she secured a job with the Central Public Health Laboratory, the UK equivalent of the Center for Disease Control. Based in the epidemiology laboratory, she worked closely with the directors of specialist microbiology laboratories and gained an understanding of the laboratory aspects of infectious disease. 'In my subsequent career,' she notes, 'I gave special attention to the laboratory aspects of my work focusing on infections in pregnancy and early childhood. I was immediately confronted by a rubella pandemic sweeping across Europe and the US in which tens of thousands of children were born with congenital abnormalities such as heart defects, cataracts and deafness. Over the subsequent decade I concentrated on unraveling the complex story of rubella and its damaging effects. One part of this was to demonstrate that vaccines worked,' she recounts. 'Live attenuated rubella vaccine was first tested in a trial in nuns and monks in closed religious communities to ensure that the vaccine virus would not spread from vaccinated to unvaccinated individuals. Permission to carry this out was granted by the Archbishop of Westminster, head of the Catholic Church in England and Wales. No doubt an important consideration was the prospect of avoiding a large number of pregnancies being terminated for rubella and the birth of children with congenital defects. Happily, this turned out to be the case as a successful rubella vaccination program was soon implemented.'

Professor Peckham describes a number of lessons that came from this experience. 'The first was the importance of being able to interact closely with colleagues in microbiology; the second crucial lesson was the importance of not only being an epidemiologist but also a clinician. In addition to being a population-based physician, I was able to set up clinics and personally examine the children who had been exposed to rubella infection in pregnancy. An important finding was that some children who were developing normal speech and language at two years were profoundly deaf at five suggesting that the virus persisted and continued to inflict damage after birth. This was important as it highlighted the need for much longer follow up of children with congenital infections and drew attention to the potential damaging consequences in adult life.' As she points out, 'there is some evidence to suggest that exposure to infections in pregnancy might cause health problems in adult life.'

'Along the way,' she relates, 'I had to develop an expertise in developmental medicine. One of my mentors was Dr. Mary Sheridan who was a pioneer in developing tools for the early assessment of vision, hearing and speech and language. Unknown to most people Mary Sheridan was also a playwright. She insisted that I examine hundreds of children under her supervision before she let me loose.'

'By the time I was 28,' she says, 'I had three children under the age of four. Around this time we lived in Paris for two years, where my husband worked as a research fellow in a cancer institute. Here I looked after my young family, wrote up the results of my research and gave flute lessons to supplement our modest grant as well as translated French scientific papers into English.'

'Returning to London I obtained a Medical Research Council fellowship in the Department of Microbiology at the Institute of Child Health. While continuing to work on infections in pregnancy I was asked to become medical advisor to the National Development Study, a unique birth cohort of 16,000 children born in one week in 1958 in England, Scotland and Wales. This yielded a rich stream of invaluable information,' she notes, 'and demonstrated starkly the impact of social, economic and environmental factors on child health and development.'

Catherine Peckham's next move was as head of a new academic department at the Charing Cross Hospital Medical School in London where, as she relates, 'I was fortunate to work closely with one of the most prominent and charismatic physicians of his time, Professor Hugh de Wardener.' She tells of how she and Professor de Wardener discovered that they had an unusual mutual acquaintance, the daughter of Elspeth Champcommunal, chief designer for Worth London who had known Monet at Giverny.

About this time *The Lancet* carried an editorial suggesting that cytomegalovirus (CMV)[1] infection in pregnancy was a major cause of mental retardation second only to Down's syndrome. The editorial concluded that pregnant women should be tested for CMV and if they acquired the infection they should be offered a termination. 'I was shocked by such a proposal,' she explains. 'The claim was enough for me to say, hang on, where is the justification? I reviewed what was known and found no evidence to support *The Lancet* statement. An ambitious project was launched to resolve the issue. A dedicated laboratory was set up at the medical school and over several years around 30,000 pregnant women and their newborns were recruited into the project. The upshot was that most women with CMV infection had normal children and the risk of abnormality was low.'

'Epidemiological studies take a long time to complete,' she explains. 'The CMV study took eight years. Given the length of time involved, people in this line of work must have patience and determination. You have to collaborate with the best laboratories, clinicians, statisticians and others. For each of these studies close collaboration is an essential ingredient.'

Catherine Peckham then returned to the Institute of Child Health at University College, where she was appointed to the UK's first established chair in paediatric epidemiology, a special initiative of the University of London. She goes on to say, 'throughout my career I have been strongly committed to the concept of an epidemiologist who is also a clinician, and the positioning of my new department as part of the UK's prime children's hospital was not just tokenistic but essential.'

The problem of AIDS was just emerging as the study on cytomegalovirus was ending and this became the focus of Catherine Peckham's research. 'We realized we needed to act very quickly,' she says, 'because we knew that most of the women with HIV weren't symptomatic and the risk of the virus passing to the infant might be very different from that of the women with AIDS. But the study couldn't be done in just one country.' She and an Italian colleague, Carlo Giaquinto, founded a ten-country European collaboration. Together the researchers designed the project so that each center in each country did the same evaluation based on a common protocol. They were able to do this because the health systems in the participating countries gave access to antenatal care with the required information captured as part of a routine visit.

It was a very successful study. 'Within a few years we had established the risk of mother-to-child infection and pinpointed some of the risk factors for viral transmission. Because of the highly successful collaboration between the participants the results were quickly taken up into practice.'

She explains that 'a unique aspect of the study was an insistence that published work be attributed not to individuals but to the European Collaborative Study. Medical journals, however, prefer to attribute authorship to an individual or individuals; doing so increases the number of times an article is cited, which is important to publishers since the number of citations is among the factors used to rank journals. We insisted!' she says. 'We wanted the credit to go to everyone. It was difficult, but in the end, we succeeded.'

Professor Peckham has also been prominent in research ethics and served as Vice-Chair of the Nuffield Council on Bioethics[2]; it is an area in which she has always had a keen interest. The ethics of doing research in developing countries, including the relationship between developed and developing countries, is also among her areas of expertise and she has served on various working groups examining these issues. 'We looked at issues around the survival and care of the vulnerable newborn baby, particularly the very premature baby. The issues are not merely medical; they involve politics, poverty and social and environmental factors, aspects that are often ignored in medicine,' she notes. 'It's important not to be cut off from what people in these spheres are thinking. I think there is a responsibility to become involved in these debates, particularly for those working with children and babies.'

Much of her work has had a global perspective. At the invitation of the French health minister she served as the Vice President of the Fonds de Solidarité Thérapeutique International, which was established to facilitate access to treatment for HIV in developing countries. In addition, she chaired the Positive Action for Children Fund,[3] which is dedicated to preventing HIV infection in children around the globe. Currently, Professor Peckham is scientific advisor to the European ZIKA virus program on infections in pregnancy and early life that is being undertaken in Jamaica, Haiti and Brazil.

Catherine Peckham reflects on the future of her area of work and sees a growing challenge. She points out that 'infectious diseases once thought to be on their way out are set to be a major threat in the future.' She chaired the Scientific Coordinating Group of the government's Foresight Programme on the Future Challenge of Infectious Diseases in humans, animals and plants, which gave stark warning of the threat posed by newly emergent infections.

A final piece of advice focuses on the perennial issue of balancing career and family. 'I had three children by the time I was 28,' Professor Peckham recounts, 'and I had to work out care for my children as well as pursuing my career. At the same time my husband was building his own career. Becoming an epidemiologist was in a sense fortuitous; I could have opted for other areas in medicine. Once the opportunity came along I soon saw that there were many research questions to which answers were needed. I think that whatever you take up can be made interesting if you engage with the issues. Based on my own experience I would advise women embarking on an academic career not to spread their energies too widely. If you focus and become an expert in a particular area this is much more fruitful. Although it was not easy I found it was possible to pursue an active career while caring for my children. From the outset, I concentrated on solving infectious disease problems. I had no inclination to invest my energies in administration at the expense of original research. That wasn't of interest to me.' She also believes it is important to find mentors and others who can provide guidance and training. 'There were certain people I sought out, for example Mary Sheridan. Throughout my career I have in turn derived enormous satisfaction acting as a mentor for clinicians and scientists, placing great emphasis on the training of young pediatricians from a range of disciplines such as respiratory medicine, intensive care and ophthalmology in epidemiology.'

'I came from a background where earlier generations of women were among the first to become doctors, politicians and academics,' she says describing her early family life. 'My father, Scientific Director of OECD, became involved in the wider aspects of science policy and co-founded the Club of Rome with Aurelio Peccei.[4] This placed me in an environment where I met people from all over the globe who were talking about environmental and other problems that are now high on the agenda, but,' she points out, '30 years ago issues such as sustainability, governance and the consequences of technological advances attracted much less attention. This milieu gave me the confidence to do something if I thought it was really important,' she states.

'I've always been very independent and assumed that I must make my own way in the world,' she continues. 'I was brought up in a disciplined, but free environment. For example, when I was 17 I biked from London to Italy with two other girls. We managed remarkably well despite having very little money. That experience and others like it reinforced my sense of independence. It helped me see things in a much broader way. I realized if you think big, you can do something little to make a big difference. It makes you understand that nothing is easy, but many things are possible,' she contends.

The self-confidence she learned as a girl was apparent from the beginning of her career. 'Early on I did a study of pregnant women and the results were questioned by a visiting American physician who claimed the doctors weren't picking up congenital malformations. I was taken aback. I was quite confident in the results, which I knew were right, so I went back and examined every child in the study. The results were correct! The thing is, his results were based on children attending hospital not the children of the population as a whole. Of course,' she adds, 'you'll find higher incidences of birth defects or other complications from pregnancy if you only look at children in hospital and exclude those in the wider community.'

LEADERSHIP STYLE

Professor Catherine Peckham is a self-confident entrepreneurial leader who defined and developed her career in medicine and research. Such entrepreneurial abilities are successful when one is knowledgeable and self-confident, two qualities Professor Peckham exudes and which were coupled with self-assurance that she was on a career path that would contribute positively to medicine and children's health.

NOTES

1. Information about cytomegalovirus is on the website of the Centers for Disease Control and Prevention and is available at https://www.cdc.gov/cmv/congenital-infection.html.
2. The Nuffield Council on Bioethics, which examines and reports on ethical issues in biology and medicine, has an international reputation for advising policymakers and fostering debate in bioethics. More information is available at http://nuffieldbioethics.org.
3. More information about the Positive Action for Children Fund is available at https://www.viivhealthcare.com/community-partnerships/positive-action-for-children-fund/about.aspx.
4. The Club of Rome, an organization of individuals formed in the late 1960s, promotes understanding of and proposes solutions to global challenges facing humanity. More information is available at https://www.clubofrome.org/about-us/.

Conclusion

'It took me quite a long time to develop a voice, and now that I have it, I am not going to be silent.' – Madeleine Albright.

If we had written this book some years ago, we might have asked the question, 'What characteristics and talents do women need to advance themselves as global leaders?' But the world has changed and despite setbacks, we find numbers of women who are fully prepared for leadership positions in a variety of settings. We have included some of these women in our study.

The women we studied, each of whom comes from a dramatically different background, have a number of characteristics in common. First, each comes from a situation or culture where women do not play dominating roles. This situation could be their culture. For example, there are almost no women leaders in industry in Japan, even though there is momentum to change that. In Jordan women have only recently received equal rights. Although there are many famous Indian women leaders, there are still numerous dangers and threats to women every day both in the large cities as well as in rural areas. In the UK, allegedly the most forward thinking of the four locations considered, only seven women serve as CEOs at FTSE 100 companies, although 26 percent of all FTSE 100 board members are now female (Cohen, 2016; Sealy et al., 2016).

Many of these women work in sectors of their political economies that have few or no other women. And they see themselves as mentors as well as leaders. Mieko Yoshida and Ryoko Nagata were the first women in Japan appointed to senior positions in large multinational Japanese companies. Nobuko Hiwasa was one of the first women to be appointed an outside director of a major Japanese company. Yukako Kurose, who fought discrimination as a married woman with children, is now a mentor and leader in the diversity movement in Japan. And soft-spoken Hisa Anan was the beneficiary of the invaluable mentorship of Nobuko Hiwasa. Reem Abu Hassan is one of the first women to sit on the Jordanian Cabinet. Jumana Ghanaimat is the first woman to run a daily newspaper in the Middle East, and outspoken Nadia Shamroukh started the first shelter for battered women in Jordan. These women are all 'firsts,' and, as exemplars, they will set models for future women leaders in Jordan.

Francesca Raleigh O'Connell spent her whole career in the UK financial sector, a sector well known for the paucity of women executives. Terrie Alafat, who worked in the British Civil Service for most of her career, talks about the need for more women in government, particularly at senior levels. Professor Catherine Peckham was one of the first women to combine a career in medicine and epidemiology in the UK. Similarly resourceful, Dr. Astrid Gajiwala was the first person to develop a tissue bank in India! All of these women display courage and fearlessness. They seem to have ignored cultural or social barriers and simply pressed on in their professions.

Corinne Kumar and Sharma Sujata are spiritual leaders, seeing their spiritual mission to help the poor and disabled. Their spirituality, while the center of their belief system, drives their practical focus on the disadvantaged. Jeroo Billimoria uses her knowledge and skills as an entrepreneur, which she could have monetized in the business community, to start multiple nonprofit ventures – nine at last count – that focus on the economic, social and educational needs of children, not only in India but also globally. She illustrates how basic business skills can be tools for child development.

Claire Jenkins, like Jeroo Billimoria, is an extraordinary leader. These two women are models for using every advantage to expand their careers. Each, in different ways, has made the most of her opportunities by taking on challenging projects without hesitation or worry about whether or not the projects will succeed.

Each of the 16 women is an exemplar for thousands of other women in public and private sectors of many economies. Each works unwaveringly toward goals that set the agenda for her projects and focus. Given that focus, each exudes self-confidence that (a) these goals are worth achieving, (b) they are viable and (c) she can achieve them.

Each woman took on projects that were well beyond what was predicted by her parents and schooling. The word 'no' seemed to have been eliminated from these women's vocabularies. Some of them, like Claire Jenkins and Jeroo Billimoria, were flexible adapting their careers to new opportunities. Others such as Terrie Alafat and Sharma Sujata were unwavering in their commitments to a single set of purposes. Each woman was a risk-taker although some might not have described themselves that way. Some saw themselves as being at the right place at the right time, inspired by luck; but without their talents and self-confidence they could not have taken up the challenge of that apparently serendipitous venture. None of them pretended to emulate a masculine style of leadership. Most importantly, each was authentic, making the most of her talents and intelligence, each worked on being inclusive and none was hypocritical.

These women are not only models for those who might share the same nationality or are working in the same field, but also for all women who aspire to leadership positions. They provide insights into how women can succeed even in difficult environments where class differences, religious taboos, and/or cultural and social mores seem to preclude their success. The stories of these successful women can provide insights for their male counterparts as well.

We have learned much from these women and their experiences. Based on this we propose the following top ten recommendations for any woman seeking to advance into a leadership position:

1. Do not sacrifice your basic values and belief system; use these to your advantage to distinguish yourself from your colleagues and competitors.
2. Be self-confident and exude that.
3. Take risks. Do not avoid taking a new position or changing jobs or careers.
4. Do not say no. You can figure it out.
5. Be yourself and create your own authentic leadership style. Do not try to act like your male counterparts.
6. Plan, plan, plan your careers and career paths, but be flexible when new opportunities arise.
7. Be transparent. There are no secrets anyway.
8. Go the extra mile. You will often have to work harder than your male colleagues. But that will be noticed.

9. Seek and/or engage in mentoring of other women and support them.
10. Work to change the workplace stereotypes about women.

Despite the plethora of qualified and talented women, it is unclear what is required to advance the progress of women in leadership positions, globally. Goal 5 of the United Nations 2030 Sustainable Development Goals is unequivocal: 'Achieve gender equality and empower all women and girls' (2015). Whether this is achievable remains to be seen, particularly in view of the unequivocal statement of the International Labour Office: 'If current trends prevail, it will take more than 70 years before gender wage gaps are closed completely' (2016, xvi).

Still, there are some very positive developments on the horizon. According to a recent article in *The Economist* there is a persistent increase in demand for women at the top of major corporations. This is not merely because of pressures to increase the diversity on boards and in executive suites. It is also because women in present leadership positions are talented, emotionally intelligent, less egoistic, more inclusive and more adaptable – all qualities needed to compete or to serve needs in a global economy. The changing demands of leadership talents are best suited to women. Their flexibility as well as their displays of altruism and optimism fit well in new political economies and in the twenty-first century focus on a more inclusive workforce (Kellaway, 2016; Adler, 1997; Lewis, 2014).

Bibliography

Abu Hassan, R. (2003), 'The laws governing the work of women in Muslim countries today: The Jordanian case', *Hawwa*, **1** (3), 351–77.

Adler, N.J. (1997), 'Global leadership: Women leaders', *Management International Review*, **37**, 171–96.

Alagaraja, M. and K. Wilson (2016), 'The confluence of individual autonomy and collective identity in India: A narrative ethnography using an Indian-U.S. sociocultural lens', *Advances in Developing Human Resources*, **18** (1), 26–37.

Albright, M. '39 famous Madeleine Albright quotes'. Available from: http://nlcatp.org/39-famous-madeleine-albright-quotes/ [Accessed 2 February 2017].

Alghad English (2014), 'Anonymous lawsuit against Ghunaimat', October 22. Available from: http://english.alghad.com/articles/832089-Anonymous-lawsuit-against-Ghunaimat [Accessed 4 October 2016].

Al-Zoubi, A.F. (2014), 'The effect of sex (gender) on the success of businesswomen in the business environment in marketing in Jordan (an empirical study)', *British Journal of Marketing Studies*, **2** (7).

APEC (2015), 'Japan women's innovative network (J-WIN)', Asia-Pacific Economic Cooperation. Available from: http://www.we-apec.com/directory/japan-women%E2%80%99s-innovative-network-j-win [Accessed 21 November 2016].

Appelbaum, S.H., B.T. Shapiro, K. Didus, T. Luongo and B. Paz (2013a), 'Upward mobility for women managers: Styles and perceptions: Part one', *Industrial and Commercial Training*, **45** (1), 51–9.

Appelbaum S.H., B.T. Shapiro, K. Didus, T. Luongo and B. Paz (2013b), 'Upward mobility for women managers: Styles and perceptions: Part two', *Industrial and Commercial Training*, **45** (2), 110–18.

Arab International Women's Forum (2012), 'Young Arab women leaders the voice of the future', AIWF 2012 Conference Series, June. Available from: http://www.aiwfonline.com/Files/Speeches AndPub/Jordan2012/AIWF_Amman_Conference_Report.pdf [Accessed 16 October 2016].

Arora, P. (2013), 'Turning problems into opportunities', Chandigarh, India: Tribune News Service, December 25. Available from: http://www.tribuneindia.com/2013/20131226/haryana.htm [Accessed 3 December 2016].

Associated Press (1996), 'Grand met to expand Burger King in Japan', March 14. Available from: http://www.apnewsarchive. com/1996/Grand-Met-To-Expand-Burger-King-In-Japan/id-2db4 90b454cb6505584b045dee6f0870 [Accessed 16 January 2017].

Auslin, M. (2015), 'Japan's gamble on "Womenomics"; Abe's drive to increase women in the workforce runs up against the need for higher birthrates', *Wall Street Journal* (Online), February 27. Available from: https://www.wsj.com/articles/michael-auslin-japans-gamble-on-womenomics-1424998266. [Accessed 25 July 2015].

Azzeh, L. (2015), 'NGO enables abused women to take control of their lives', *The Jordan Times*, December 1. Available from: http://www.jordantimes.com/news/local/ngo-enables-abused-women-take-control-their-lives [Accessed 25 October 2016].

Azzeh, L. (2016), 'Gov't "committed to legal amendments to protect women" – minister', *The Jordan Times*, August 30. Available from: http://www.jordantimes.com/news/local/gov't-committed-legal-amendments-protect-women'---minister [Accessed 25 October 2016].

Babu, V. (2011), 'Divergent leadership styles practiced by global managers in India', *Indian Journal of Industrial Relations*, **46** (3), 478–90.

Bagati, D. and N.M. Carter (2010), *Leadership Gender Gap in India Inc.: Myths and Realities*. Catalyst. Available from: http://www.catalyst.org/system/files/Leadership_Gap_in_India_Inc._Myths_and_Realities.pdf [Accessed 2 August 2016].

Baker, A. (2005), 'Growing talent is everybody's business', *Journal of Accountancy*, **200** (3), 90–1.

Baker, C. (2014), 'Stereotyping and women's roles in leadership positions', *Industrial and Commercial Training*, **46** (6), 332–7.

Bakshi, S.K. (2011), 'Trade liberalization in India: Impact on gender segregation', Delhi: The Energy and Resources Institute,

July. Available from: http://www.isid.ac.in/~pu/conference/dec_ 11_conf/Papers/ShilpiKapurBakshi.pdf [Accessed 16 September 2016].

Bannigan, D. (2016), 'Can we help boardrooms find an untapped reservoir of talented women?', *Huffpost Business United Kingdom*, June 4. Available from: http://www.huffingtonpost.co. uk/harriet-lamb/breaking-through-glass-borders_b_3364304.html [Accessed 11 November 2016].

Barcucci, V. and N. Mryyan (2014), 'Labour market transitions of young women and men in Jordan', Geneva: ILO, June. Available from: http://www.ilo.org/wcmsp5/groups/public/—dgreports/—dcomm/documents/publication/wcms_245876.pdf [Accessed 16 October 2016].

Bass, B. (1998), *Transformational Leadership*. New York: Erlbaum Associates.

Batra, R. and T.G. Reio (2016), 'Gender inequality issues in India', *Advances in Developing Human Resources*, **18** (1), 88–101.

Beasley, A.L. (2005), 'The style split,' *Journal of Accountancy*, **200** (3), 91–2.

Beninger, A. and N.M. Carter (2013), 'The great debate: Flexibility vs. FaceTime: Busting the myths behind flexible work arrangements', New York: Catalyst. Available from: http://www.catalyst. org/system/files/the_great_debate_flexibility_vs_face_time.pdf [Accessed 20 June 2016].

Bennett, A. (2013), 'Women feel they'd be further in their career "if more confident"', *Huffington Business United Kingdom*, August 16. Available from: http://www.huffingtonpost.co.uk/2013/08/16/ women-glass-ceiling_n_3766593.html [Accessed 19 September 2016].

Bhattacharya, A., R. Srivastava and N. Jain (2010), *Indian Manufacturing: The Next Growth Orbit*. Boston Consulting Group, January. Available from: http://www.bcg.de/documents/file 73668.pdf [Accessed 2 August 2016].

Block, C.J., S.M. Koch, B.E. Liberman, T.J. Merriweather and L. Roberson (2011), 'Contending with stereotype threat at work: A model of long-term responses', *The Counseling Psychologist*, **39** (4), 570–600.

Bolton, S.C. (2015), 'Why there are so many women managers, but so few women CEOs', *The Conversation*, United Kingdom edition, March 6. Available from: https://theconversation.com/

why-there-are-so-many-women-managers-but-so-few-women-ceos-38447 [Accessed 20 November 2016].
Buechel, B. (2015), 'Women on boards', *Leadership Excellence*, **32** (8), 10.
Burns, J.M. (2003), *Transforming Leadership*. New York: Grove Press.
Caliper Research & Development Department (2014), 'Women leaders research paper'. Available from: https://www.calipercorp.com/home-3/banner-women-leaders-white-paper/ [Accessed 18 May 2016].
Carter, N.M., H. Foust-Cummings, L. Mulligan-Ferry and R. Soares (2013), *High Potentials in the Pipeline: On Their Way to the Boardroom*. Catalyst. Available from: http://www.catalyst.org/system/files/high_potentials_in_the_pipeline_on_their_way_to_the_boardroom.pdf [Accessed 17 June 2016].
Casad, D.J. and W.J. Bryant (2016), 'Addressing stereotype threat is critical to diversity and inclusion in organizational psychology', *Frontiers in Psychology*, **7** (8), 8–25.
Catalyst (2014), 'The case for gender diversity in Japan', New York: Catalyst, Inc., June 16. Available from: http://www.catalyst.org/knowledge/infographic-case-gender-diversity-japan [Accessed 19 July 2016].
Catalyst (2016), 'Quick take: Women in the labour force in the UK', New York: Catalyst, Inc., August 9. Available from: http://www.catalyst.org/knowledge/women-workforce-uk [Accessed 25 October 2016].
Catalyst Information Center (2012), 'India: The case for gender diversity', Catalyst, Inc., January. Available from: http://www.catalyst.org/knowledge/india-case-gender-diversity-0 [Accessed 2 August 2016].
Chamberlain, A. (2016a), 'Demystifying the gender pay gap: Evidence from glassdoor salary data', Mill Valley, CA: Glassdoor, March. Available from: https://www.glassdoor.com/research/studies/gender-pay-gap/ [Accessed 25 October 2016].
Chamberlain, A. (2016b), 'Why transparency matters for gender pay equity glassdoor', Glassdoor Economic Research Blog, April 12. Available from: https://www.glassdoor.com/research/glassdoor-nyc-roundtable/ [Accessed 25 October 2016].
Child Helpline International. Available from: www.childhelplineinternational.org

Ciulla, J., M. Uhl-Bien and P. Werhane (eds) (2013), *Leadership Ethics*, three volumes. Los Angeles: Sage Publications.

Cohen, C. (2016), 'Just who are the 7 women bosses of the FTSE 100?' *The Telegraph*, September 20. Available from: http://www.telegraph.co.uk/women/work/just-who-are-the-7-women-bosses-of-the-ftse-100/ [Accessed 12 January 2017].

Collier, J. and R. Esteban (2000), 'Systemic leadership: Ethical and effective', *Leadership & Organization Development Journal*, **21** (4), 207–15, reprinted in Ciulla et al., volume 3, 199–213.

Collins, J.C. and Y. Abichandani (2016), 'Change in the face of resistance: Positioning hope for women returnees to the Indian workforce', *Advances in Developing Human Resources*, **18** (1), 11–25.

Conger, J. and R. Kanungo (1998), *Charismatic Leadership in Organizations*. Los Angeles: Sage Publications.

Coogle, A. (2016), 'Recorded "honor" killings on the rise in Jordan', Human Rights Watch, October 27. Available from: https://www.hrw.org/news/2016/10/27/recorded-honor-killings-rise-jordan [Accessed 30 November 2016].

Cooke, F.L. and D.S. Saini (2010), 'Diversity management in India: A study of organizations in different ownership forms and industrial sectors', *Human Resource Management*, **49** (3), 477–500.

Cooley, A. (2006), 'Ivan Illich', *Encyclopedia Britannica*. Available from: https://www.britannica.com/biography/Ivan-Illich [Accessed 16 December 2016].

Cooper, C. and Y. Hagiwara (2014), 'Japan's OT culture thwarting PM's plans; long days hurting pledge to put more women into management', *Edmonton Journal*, August 2.

Cordes, S. (2015a), 'Gender equality is a sound investment', Copenhagen: Danish Centre for Gender, Equality and Diversity, October 3. Available from: http://kvinfo.org/web-magazine/gender-equality-sound-investment [Accessed 3 October 2016].

Cordes, S. (2015b), 'Jordan's well-educated women stay in the home', Copenhagen: Danish Centre for Gender, Equality and Diversity, June 16. Available from: http://kvinfo.org/print/node/3654 [Accessed 3 October 2016].

Darnell, D. and O. Gadiesh (2013), 'Gender equality in the UK: The next stage of the journey', Bain & Company, Inc. Available from: http://www.bain.com/Images/BAIN_BRIEF_Gender_equality_in_the_UK.pdf [Accessed 25 October 2016].

Davidson, L. (2014), 'Why Shinzo Abe is right to focus on women', *The Daily Telegraph*, September 4, 10.

de Valk, P. (2014), 'Developing women into leadership positions', Blog *Huffpost Lifestyle United Kingdom*, January 23. Available from: http://www.huffingtonpost.co.uk/penny-de-valk/women-leadership_b_4181492.html [Accessed 19 September 2015].

Debusscher, P. (2015), *Evaluation of the Beijing Platform for Action +20 and the Opportunities for Achieving Gender Equality and the Empowerment of Women in the Post-2015 Development Agenda: Study for the FEMM Committee*, Brussels: European Parliament, March. Report number: PE 519.191. Available from: doi 10.2861/770907 [Accessed 14 June 2016].

Deloitte Global Center for Corporate Governance (2015), *Women in the Boardroom: A Global Perspective 4th Edition*, Deloitte Global Center for Corporate Governance. Available from: https://www2.deloitte.com/content/dam/Deloitte/global/Documents/Risk/gx-ccg-women-in-the-boardroom-a-global-perspective4.pdf [Accessed 17 June 2016].

Deutsche Gesellschaft für Internationale Zusammenarbeit (2015), 'Employment of young women through gender diversity management in companies in the MENA region', Deutsche Gesellschaft für Internationale Zusammenarbeit (GIZ) GmbH. Available from: https://www.giz.de/en/worldwide/37953.html# [Accessed 17 October 2016].

Dobbs, R., J. Manyika and J. Woetzel (2015), *The Power of Parity: Advancing Women's Equality in India*. McKinsey Global Institute, November. Available from: http://www.mckinsey.com/global-themes/employment-and-growth/the-power-of-parity-advancing-womens-equality-in-india [Accessed 19 September 2016].

Duncan, E. (2015), 'Board equality is a struggle for Japan's "womenomics"', *Financial Times*, June 29.

Duraisamy, M. and P. Duraisamy (2014), 'Occupational segregation, wage and job discrimination against women across social groups in the Indian labor market: 1983–2010', preliminary draft of conference paper. Available from: https://www.aeaweb.org/conference/2015/retrieve.php?pdfid=1028 [Accessed 16 September 2016].

Dustin, M. (2006), *Gender Equality, Cultural Diversity: European Comparisons and Lessons*, Project Report, Gender Institute, London School of Economics and Political Science. Available from: http://sro.sussex.ac.uk/64051/1/NuffieldReport_final.pdf [Accessed 19 July 2016].

Dutt, K.G. (2000), 'It aims to bring disabled into mainstream', Chandigarh, India: Tribune News Service, March 10. Available from: http://www.tribuneindia.com/2000/20000310/haryana.htm #11 [Accessed 3 December 2016].

Eagly, A.H. (2007), 'Female leadership advantage and disadvantage: Resolving the contradictions', *Psychology of Women Quarterly*, **31** (1), 1–12.

Eagly, A.H. and M.C. Johannesen-Schmidt (2001), 'The leadership styles of women and men', *Journal of Social Issues*, **57** (4), 781–97.

EcoBalance (2016), '12th Biennial International Conference', Available from: http://www.ecobalance2016.org/submission/awardee.html [Accessed 17 February 2017].

Eisner, S. (2013), 'Leadership: Gender and executive style', *S.A.M. Advanced Management Journal*, **78** (1), 26–41.

European Commission Directorate-General Justice (2013), 'The current situation of gender equality in the United Kingdom: Country profile', European Commission Directorate-General Justice, Unit D2. Available from: http://ec.europa.eu/justice/gender-equality/files/epo_campaign/130911_country-profile_united_kingdom.pdf [Accessed 12 August 2016].

European Women's Lobby (2015), *1995–2015 From Words to Action: 20 Years of the Beijing Platform for Action*, European Women's Lobby. Available from: http://www.womenlobby.org/From-words-to-action-women-can-t-wait-20-more-years-to-enjoy-their-full-human-6909 [Accessed 15 June 2016].

EY (2016), *Navigating Disruption Without Gender Diversity? Think Again*, EY, EYG Report no. 00758-164Gbl. Available from: http://www.ey.com/GL/en/Issues/Business-environment/ey-women-in-industry [Accessed 14 June 2016].

Fackler, M. (2007), 'Career women in Japan find a blocked path', *The New York Times*, August 6. Available from: http://www.nytimes.com/2007/08/06/world/asia/06equal.html [Accessed 22 July 2015].

Fackler, M. and M. McDonald (2011), 'Japan pushes to rescue survivors as quake toll rises', *The New York Times*, March 12. Available from: http://mwr.gtm.nytimes.com/2011/03/13/world/asia/13japan.html [Accessed 22 July 2015].

Fisk, R. (2015), 'A place of refuge from fear and guilt', *The Independent*, September 9. Available from: http://www.independent.co.uk/voices/commentators/fisk/robert-fisk-a-place-of-refuge-from-fear-and-guilt-2075213.html [Accessed 28 January 2017].

Folke Bernadotte Academy (2015), 'About FBA', Sandöverken, Sweden: Folke Bernadotte Academy. Available from https://fba.se/en/about-fba/ [Accessed 19 January 2017].

Freedom House (2015), 'Country report: Jordan'. Available from: https://freedomhouse.org/report/freedom-world/2015/jordan [Accessed 16 October 2016].

Friedman, S., D. Laurison and A. Miles (2015), 'Breaking the "class" ceiling? Social mobility into Britain's elite occupations', *The Sociological Review*, **63** (2), 259–89.

Friedman, T. (2005), *The World is Flat*, New York: Farrar, Strauss and Giroux.

Garg, S. and S. Jain (2013), 'Mapping leadership styles of public and private sector leaders using Blake and Mouton leadership model', *Drishtikon: A Management Journal*, **4** (1), 48–64.

'Gender equality and inclusion in Jordan's private sector'. Copenhagen: Danish Centre for Gender, Equality and Diversity. Available from: http://kvinfo.org/mena/gender-equality-and-inclusion-jordans-private-sector [Accessed 3 October 2016].

'Gender in work project', Amman, Jordan: Business Development Center. Available from: http://www.bdc.org.jo/Gender_in_Work_Project.aspx [Accessed 17 October 2016].

Ghazal, M. (2014a), 'Case against Al Ghad chief editor dismissed', *The Jordan Times*, October 29. Available from: http://www.jordantimes.com/news/local/case-against-al-ghad-chief-editor-dismissed [Accessed 23 November 2016].

Ghazal, M. (2014b), 'Press association stands behind Al Ghad chief editor', *The Jordan Times*, October 22. Available from: http://www.jordantimes.com/news/local/press-association-stands-behind-al-ghad-chief-editor [Accessed 23 November 2016].

Ghosh, R. (2016), 'Gender and diversity in India: Contested territories for HRD?', *Advances in Developing Human Resources*, **18** (1), 3–10.

Ghunaimat, J. (2014), 'A message to anonymous', Amman, Jordan: Alghad English, November 1. Available from: http://69.162.64.182/articles/834046-A-message-to-anonymous?s=82c1e7a4317fb3aeab993062623aca4b [Accessed 15 December 2016].

Gilligan, C. (1977), 'In a different voice: Women's conceptions of self and morality', reprinted from *Harvard Educational Review*, **47**, 481–92 and 509–17 in J. Ciulla et al., volume 2, 286–306.

Gilligan, C. (1982), *In a Different Voice: Psychological Theory and Women's Development*. Cambridge, MA: Harvard University Press.

Global Thinkers Forum (2012), 'Women leaders in MENA: Power & creativity', Amman, Jordan. Available from: http://www.globalthinkersforum.org/wp-content/uploads/2013/02/GTF-Women-Leaders-in-MENA-LRe1.pdf [Accessed 17 October 2016].

Goth, A.F. (2010), 'The delicate balance between children and careers', Copenhagen: Danish Centre for Gender, Equality and Diversity, August 25. Available from: http://kvinfo.org/mena/delicate-balance-between-children-and-careers [Accessed 3 October 2016].

Goussous, S. (2015), 'Business leaders call for enhancing women's economic participation', *Jordan Times*, November 16. Available from: http://www.jordantimes.com/news/local/business-leaders-call-enhancing-women's-economic-participation [Accessed 4 October 2016].

Government Equalities Office (2015), 'Think, Act, Report framework', London: Government Equalities Office, July 15. Available from: https://www.gov.uk/government/publications/think-act-report-measures/think-act-report-framework [Accessed 20 November 2016].

Government Equalities Office (2016), 'Trailblazing transparency: Mending the gap', London: Government Equalities Office, February 9. Available from: https://www.gov.uk/government/publications/trailblazing-transparency-report-on-closing-the-gender-pay-gap [Accessed 20 November 2016].

Grant Thornton International Ltd. (2016), *Women in Business: Turning Promise into Practice*. Available from: http://www.grantthornton.global/insights/articles/women-in-business-2016/ [Accessed 17 June 2016].

Greenberg, H.M. and P.J. Sweeney (2005a), 'How women are redefining leadership', Princeton, NJ: Caliper Corporation. Available from: http://www.calipermedia.calipercorp.com/articles/us/how-women-are-redefining-leadership.pdf [Accessed 25 July 2016].

Greenberg, H.M. and P.J. Sweeney (2005b), 'Leadership: Qualities that distinguish women', *Financial Executive*, **21** (6), 32–6.

Greenleaf, R. (1977; 2002), *Servant Leadership*, Mahwah, NJ: Paulist Press.

Griffen, V. (2008), 'Discussing gender and international cultural relations', The British Council. Available from: https://www.britishcouncil.org/sites/default/files/gender_and_icr.pdf [Accessed 19 July 2016].

Groysberg, B., Y-J. Cheng and D. Bell (2016), *2016 Global Board of Directors Survey*, Spencer Stuart and WCD Foundation. Available from: https://www.spencerstuart.com/research-and-insight/2016-global-board-of-directors-survey [Accessed 17 June 2016].

Harvey, S. (2015), 'Transcultural women leaders', *S.A.M. Advanced Management Journal*, **80** (1), 12–19, 50.

Hays Asia (2016), 'Power female ambition: Develop career opportunities', *Global Gender Diversity Report 2016*, Hays Asia. Available from: http://www.hays.co.jp/cs/groups/hays_common/@jp/documents/webassets/hays_1307062.pdf [Accessed 16 October 2016].

Heideman, K., C. Nietsche, J. Craig Romano, E. White, M. Fetterly and E. Parker (eds) (2014), *Beijing+20: Looking Back and the Road Ahead*, Washington, DC: Woodrow Wilson International Center for Scholars. Available from: https://www.wilsoncenter.org/publication/beijing20-looking-back-and-the-road-ahead [Accessed 14 June 2016].

Husseini, R. (2016a), 'New projected shelter to house women under threat over "family honour"', *The Jordan Times*, December 3. Available from: http://www.jordantimes.com/news/local/new-projected-shelter-house-women-under-threat-over-family-honour' [Accessed December 15, 2016].

Husseini, R. (2016b), 'Second sister shot in Naour "honour crime" dies', *The Jordan Times*, October 16. Available from: http://www.jordantimes.com/news/local/second-sister-shot-naour-honour-crime'-dies [Accessed 15 December 2016].

Iinuma, A. and C. Black (2014), *A More Diverse Workplace: Increasing Women's Power in Japan*, Heidrick & Struggles International, Inc. Available from: http://www.heidrick.com/~/media/Publications%20and%20Reports/Increasing-Women-Power-in-Japan.pdf [Accessed 19 July 2016].

Institute for Human Development (2014), *India Labour and Employment Report, 2014: Highlights*, New Delhi: Academic Foundation. Available from: http://www.ihdindia.org/ILERpdf/Highlights%20of%20the%20Report.pdf [Accessed 26 July].

Institute of Leadership and Management (2011), 'Ambition and gender at work', London, Institute of Leadership & Management. Available from: https://www.i-l-m.com/About-ILM/Research-programme/Research-reports/Ambition-and-gender [Accessed 20 November 2016].

International Finance Corporation (2013), *Investing in Women's Employment: Good for Business, Good for Development*, Washington, DC: International Finance Corporation. Available from: http://www.ifc.org/wps/wcm/connect/5f6e5580416bb016bfb1bf9e78015671/InvestinginWomensEmployment.pdf?MOD=AJPERES [Accessed 19 July 2016].

International Finance Corporation (2015), *Gender Diversity in Jordan*, Washington, DC: International Finance Corporation. Available from: http://www.ifc.org/wps/wcm/connect/topics_ext_content/ifc_external_corporate_site/corporate+governance/publications/gender+diversity+in+jordan [Accessed 28 June 2016].

International Labour Office (2015), *Women in Business and Management: Gaining Momentum*, Geneva: International Labour Office. Available from: http://www.ilo.org/global/publications/ilo-bookstore/order-online/books/WCMS_316450/lang--en/index.htm ISBN 978-92-2-128874-9 (web pdf) [Accessed 20 June 2016].

International Labour Office (2016), *Women at Work: Trends 2016*, Geneva: International Labour Office. Available from: http://www.ilo.org/gender/Informationresources/Publications/WCMS_457317/lang--en/index.htm [Accessed 20 June 2016].

Jaishankar, D. (2013), 'The huge cost of India's discrimination against women', *The Atlantic*, March 18. Available from: http://www.theatlantic.com/international/archive/2013/03/the-huge-cost-of-indias-discrimination-against-women/274115/ [Accessed 17 September 2016].

Jamieson, P. (2010), 'What's a girl to do?', *Development and Learning in Organizations: An International Journal*, **24** (5), 36–8.

Japan Tobacco Inc. (2015a), 'Annual report 2015', Tokyo: Japan Tobacco Inc. Available from: https://www.jt.com/investors/results/annual_report/pdf/annual.fy2015_E_all.pdf [Accessed 5 December 2016].

Japan Tobacco Inc. (2015b), 'JT group sustainability report FY2015', Tokyo: Japan Tobacco Inc. Available from: https://

www.jt.com/csr/report/pdf/JT_Group_Sustainability_Report_FY 2015_web.pdf [Accessed 5 December 2016].

Jordan Ahli Bank (2015), 'Jordan Ahli Bank expands the partner network of its Nashmeyat initiative', *Jordan Ahli Bank News*, March. Available from: http://ahli.com/en/jordan/general/news/jordan-ahli-bank-expands-partner-network-its-nashmeyat-initiative-signing [Accessed 17 October 2016].

Jordan Business (2015), 'Top 20 companies to work for in Jordan: The results are in', September. Available from: http://www.jordanbusinessmagazine.com/cover_story/top-20-companies-work-jordan-results-are [Accessed 17 October 2016].

Jordan Media Guide (2017), Available from: https://sites.google.com/site/jordanmediaguide/Jordanian-arabic-newspapers [Accessed 5 January 2017].

Jordanian National Commission for Women (2011), 'National report progress of Jordanian women: In pursuit of justice, participation and equality 2010–2011'. Available from: http://haqqi.info/en/haqqi/research/national-report-progress-jordanian-women-pursuit-justice-participation-and-equality [Accessed 16 October 2016].

Jordanian Women's Union (2016), Available from: http://jwu.org.jo/home.aspx?lng=1 [Accessed 15 December 2016].

Kawakami, C., J.B. White and E.J. Langer (2000), 'Mindful and masculine: Freeing women leaders from the constraints of gender roles', *Journal of Social Issues*, **56** (1), 49–63.

Kelan, E. (2015), *Men Middle Managers and Gender Inclusive Leadership*, Cranfield International Centre for Women Leaders. Available from: http://www.som.cranfield.ac.uk/som/p24658/Research/Research-Centres/Cranfield-International-Centre-for-Women-Leaders/Gender-Inclusive-Leadership [Accessed 22 June 2016].

Kellaway, L. (2016), 'Women take charge: A power shift in the boardroom', *The Economist*. Available from: http://www.theworldin.com/article/12762/women-take-charge?fsrc=scn/tw/wi/bl/ed/ [Accessed 22 June 2016].

Kennedy, J.F. (1962), 'Special message to the congress on protecting the consumer interest', The American Presidency Project, March 15. Available from: http://www.presidency.ucsb.edu/ws/?pid=9108 [Accessed 26 January 2017].

Konner, M. (2015), 'A better world, run by women; male biology has brought the world war, corruption and scandal, Women are poised to lead us to a better place', *Wall Street Journal* (Online), March 6. Available from: https://www.wsj.com/articles/a-better-world-run-by-women-1425657910 [Accessed 14 June 2016].

Kumar, C. (2007), *Asking, We Walk: The South as New Political Imaginary*, Volume I, Bangalore, India: Streelekha Publications.

Kumar, C. (2011), *Asking, We Walk: The South as New Political Imaginary*, Volume II, Bangalore, India: Streelekha Publications.

Kumar, C. (2012), *Asking, We Walk: The South as New Political Imaginary*, Volume III, Bangalore, India: Streelekha Publications.

Kumar, C. (2013), *Asking, We Walk: The South as New Political Imaginary*, Volume IV, Bangalore, India: Streelekha Publications.

Kurmanath, K.V. (2012), 'Comeback women', *The Hindu*. Available from: http://www.thehindu-businessline.com/features/weekend-life/comeback-women/article3985077.ece [Accessed 22 September 2016].

Lamb, H. (2013), 'Breaking through glass borders', *HuffPost UK Women*, July 31 (online). Available from: www.huffingtonpost.co.uk/harriet-lamb/breaking-through-glass-borders_b_3364304.html [Accessed 25 October 2016].

Lewis, G. (2014), 'Gen Y women will be first to break glass ceiling, research predicts', *People Management*, October 13. Available from: http://www2.cipd.co.uk/pm/peoplemanagement/b/weblog/archive/2014/10/13/gen-y-females-will-be-first-to-break-glass-ceiling-research-predicts.aspx [Accessed 16 July 2016].

Lewis, L. (2016), 'Abe "Womenomics" programme looks all at sea', *Financial Times*, June 4. Available from: http://proxy.library.georgetown.edu/login?url=http://search.proquest.com/docview/1801523015?accountid=11091 [Accessed 18 August 2016].

Llewellyn Consulting (2016), *Which Countries in Europe Have the Best Gender Equality in the Workplace?*, Research Report, Mill Valley, CA: Glassdoor. May. Available from: https://blog-content.glassdoor.com/app/uploads/sites/9/2016/05/GenderEquality_Draft3.pdf [Accessed 16 July 2016].

Lord Davies of Abersoch, Steering Committee (2011), 'Women on boards', February 24. Ref: BIS/11/745. Available from: https://www.gov.uk/government/uploads/system/uploads/attachment_data/file/31480/11-745-women-on-boards.pdf [Accessed 18 August 2016].

Lord Davies of Abersoch, Steering Committee (2015), 'Women on boards: Davies review annual report 2015', October 29. Ref: BIS/15/585. Available from: https://www.gov.uk/government/

uploads/system/uploads/attachment_data/file/415454/bis-15-134-women-on-boards-2015-report.pdf [Accessed 18 August 2016].

Martin, S.M., S. Jahani and K. Rosenblatt (2016), 'Educating young women to be global leaders: A model', *VOLUNTAS: International Journal of Voluntary and Nonprofit Organizations*, **27** (3), 1494–511.

Matanle, P., K. Ishiguro and L. McCann (2014), 'Popular culture and workplace gendering among varieties of capitalism: Working women and their representation in Japanese Manga', *Gender, Work & Organization*, **21** (5), 472–89.

Mavin, S., G. Grandy and J. Williams (2014), 'Experiences of women elite leaders doing gender: Intra-gender micro-violence between women', *British Journal of Management*, **25** (3), 439–55.

McCann, M. and S. Wheeler (2011), 'Gender diversity in the FTSE 100: The business case claim explored', *Journal of Law and Society*, **38** (4), 542–74.

McKelvey, C. (2005), 'Leader: Everyone needs powerful women', *Precision Marketing*. Available from: http://proxy.library.georgetown.edu/login?url=http://search.proquest.com/docview/217937322?accountid=11091 [Accessed 26 July 2016].

McKinsey & Company (2008), *Female Leadership, a Competitive Edge for the Future*, McKinsey & Company. Available from: http://www.mckinsey.com/global-themes/women-matter [Accessed 25 October 2016].

McKinsey & Company (2013), *Gender Diversity in Top Management: Moving Corporate Culture, Moving Boundaries*. Available from: http://www.mckinsey.com/global-themes/women-matter [Accessed 22 June 2016].

MEMRI Middle East (2015), 'Editor of Jordanian Daily Jumana Ghunaimat: Forcing women to wear the Hijab infringes on their freedom', Washington, DC: Media Research Institute, September 2. Available from: www.memri.org/report/en/0/0/0/0/0/0/8727.htm [Accessed 23 October 2016].

Milner, S. (2015), 'Made in Britain: How the UK became a worse place for women to work', *The Conversation*, United Kingdom edition, January 28. Available from: http://theconversation.com/made-in-britain-how-the-uk-became-a-worse-place-for-women-to-work-36794 [Accessed 20 November 2016].

Milovanovitch, M. (2016), 'Increasing female participation in employment through vocational education and training in Jordan', PRIME Issues Working Paper, European Training Foundation. Available from: http://www.etf.europa.eu/web.nsf/pages/PRIME_issues_paper_Jordan [Accessed 3 October 2016].

Munn, S.L. and S. Chaudhuri (2016), 'Work-life balance: A cross-cultural review of dual-earner couples in India and the United States', *Advances in Developing Human Resources*, **18** (1), no. 1, 54–68.

Nag, D. (2016), 'For women living alone in Delhi, security concerns heightened', Washington, DC: The Asia Foundation, March 2. Available from: http://asiafoundation.org/2016/03/02/for-women-living-alone-in-delhi-security-concerns-heightened/ [Accessed 17 September 2016].

Nanton, C.R. (2015), 'Shaping leadership culture to sustain future generations of women leaders', *Journal of Leadership, Accountability and Ethics*, **12** (3), 92–112.

National Statistical Commission (2012), 'Report of the committee on unorganised sector statistics', National Statistical Commission Government of India, February. Available from: http://mospi.nic.in/Mospi_New/upload/nsc_report_un_sec_14mar12.pdf [Accessed 26 July 2016].

Nemoto, K. (2013), 'When culture resists progress: Masculine organizational culture and its impacts on the vertical segregation of women in Japanese companies', *Work, Employment & Society*, **27** (1), 153–69.

O'Connor, M. (2013), 'A brief history of Taylor Swift's "Special Place in Hell for Women"', *New York Magazine*, March 6. Available from: http://nymag.com/thecut/2013/03/brief-history-of-taylor-swifts-hell-quote.html [Accessed 25 October 2016].

OECD (2013), *OECD Economic Surveys: United Kingdom 2013*, OECD Publishing. Available from: http://dx.doi.org/10.1787/eco_surveys-gbr-2013-en [Accessed 11 November 2016].

Olchawski, J. (2016), 'Sex equality: State of the nation 2016', London: Fawcett Society, January. Available from: http://www.fawcettsociety.org.uk/wp-content/uploads/2016/01/Sex-equality-state-of-the-nation-230116.pdf [Accessed 11 November 2016].

O'Neil, D.A. (2015), 'A framework for developing women leaders: Applications to executive coaching', *Journal of Applied Behavioral Science*, **51** (2), 253–76.

Painter-Morland, M. (2011), 'Systemic leadership, gender, organization' in P. Werhane and M. Painter-Morland (eds) *Leadership, Gender, and Organization*. Dordrecht, Netherlands: Springer-Verlag, 139–65.

Permanent Mission of the United States of America to the United Nations and Other International Organizations in Geneva (2014), *United States Report on the Implementation of the Beijing Declaration and Platform for Action*, Geneva: Permanent Mission of the United States of America to the United Nations and Other International Organizations in Geneva, November 5. Available from: https://geneva.usmission.gov/2014/11/05/u-s-report-on-implementation-of-the-beijing-declaration-and-platform-for-action-beijing20/ [Accessed 15 June 2016].

Pluess, J.D., A. Mohapatra, K. Fritz, C. Oger, K. Gallo and R. Meiers (2015), *Building Effective Women's Economic Empowerment Strategies*, International Center for Research on Women, 2015. Available from: http://www.icrw.org/publications/building-effective-womens-economic-empowerment-strategies [Accessed 15 June 2016].

PricewaterhouseCoopers (2015), 'Igniting change: Building the pipeline of female leaders in energy', London: PricewaterhouseCoopers Legal LLP. Available from: http://www.pwc.co.uk/industries/oil-gas/insights/focus-on-women-in-power-addressing-gender-diversity-across-energy.html [Accessed 20 November 2016].

PricewaterhouseCoopers (2016), 'Igniting change 2: Building the pipeline of female leaders in energy', London: PricewaterhouseCoopers Legal LLP. Available from: http://www.pwc.co.uk/industries/oil-gas/insights/powerful-women-igniting-change-2.html [Accessed 20 November 2016].

Pryce, P. and R. Sealy (2013), 'Promoting women to MD in investment banking: Multi-level influences', *Gender in Management: An International Journal*, **28** (8), 448–67.

Raghall, K. (2015), 'Women's rights are not about charity', *Kvinna till Kvinna*. Available from: http://kvinnatillkvinna.se/en/2015/08/10/womens-rights-are-not-about-charity/ [Accessed 22 October 2016].

Rai, S. (2012a), 'Gender diversity in boardrooms: Comparative global review and India', *Journal of Strategic Human Resource Management*, **1** (2), 16–24.

Rai, S. (2012b), 'Human resource management and labour relations in the Indian industrial sector', WZB Discussion Paper, no. SP III 2012-301. Available from: http://hdl.handle.net/10419/57096 [Accessed 27 July 2016].

Rai, S. (2013), 'Re-thinking workforce diversity in the context of India', *Journal of Strategic Human Resource Management*, **2** (2), 1–10.

Risner, E. (2012), 'Business women's network spotlight: Jordan', Business and Professional Women Association – Amman, July 12. Available from: http://thewaywomenwork.com/2012/07/business-womens-network-spotlight-jordan/ [Accessed 4 October 2016].

Roberts, G.S. (2011), 'Salary women and family well-being in urban Japan', *Marriage & Family Review*, **47** (8), 571–89.

Rosener, J.B. (1990), 'Ways women lead', *Harvard Business Review*, **68** (6), 119–25.

RSA Group (2012), 'Women on boards: A life sciences' perspective', Hatfield, Hertfordshire, UK: RSA Group. Available from: https://blogit.realwire.com/media/Women_on_Boards_RSA_Report-final.pdf [Accessed 25 October 2016].

Ruderman, M.N. and P.J. Ohlott (2005), 'Leading roles: What coaches of women need to know', *Leadership in Action*, **25** (3), 3–9.

Rustagi, P., D. Nathan, A. Datta and A. George (2013), 'Women and work in South Asia: Changes and challenges', New Delhi: Institute for Human Development. Available from: http://www.ihdindia.org/Working-Papers.html [Accessed 17 September 2016].

SAMENA Telecommunications Council (2015), 'Umniah signs the UN global women's economic empowerment principles', December 8. Available from: https://www.samenacouncil.org/samena_daily_news.php?news=56773 [Accessed 17 October 2016].

Sandler, C. (2014), 'Developing female leaders: Helping women reach the top', *Industrial and Commercial Training*, **46** (2), 61–7.

Sankaran, K. and R. Madhav (2011), *Gender Equality and Social Dialogue in India*, Geneva: International Labor Organization, January. Available from: http://www.ilo.org/wcmsp5/groups/public/---dgreports/---gender/documents/publication/wcms_1504 28.pdf [Accessed 28 July 2016].

Sayed, S. (2013), 'Can you define success?', *Huffpost Business United Kingdom*, May 8. Available from: http://www.huffington

post.co.uk/shaheen-sayed/can-you-define-success_b_2836230.html [Accessed 19 September 2016].
Schermerhorn, J., J. Hunt, R. Osborn and M. Uhl-Bien (2010), *Organizational Behavior* (11th ed.), Hoboken, NJ: John Wiley & Sons Inc.
Schram, B. (2016), 'International Women's Day 2016: The six women smashing the glass ceiling at UK's top firms', *International Business Times*, March 8. Available from: http://www.ibtimes.co.uk/international-womens-day-2016-six-women-smashing-glass-ceiling-uks-top-firms-1548219 [Accessed 19 September 2016].
Sealy, R., E. Doldor and S. Vinnicombe (2016), *The Female FTSE Board Report 2016*, Cranfield International Centre for Women Leaders. Available from: https://www.cranfield.ac.uk/press/news-2016/women-on-boards-ftse-100-company-has-full-gender-balance-for-first-time [Accessed 25 October 2016].
Sharma, S. and P. Sehrawat (2014), 'Glass ceiling for women: Does it exist in the modern India?', *Journal of Organisation and Human Behaviour*, **3** (2), 9–15.
Shriberg, A. and D. Shriberg (2011), *Practicing Leadership Principles and Applications*, Hoboken, NJ: John Wiley and Sons.
Shyamsunder, A. and M.N. Carter (2014). 'High potentials under high pressure India's technology sector', *Catalyst*. Retrieved from: http://www.catalyst.org/system/files/high_potentials_under_high_pressure_in_indias_technology_sector_0.pdf [Accessed 2 August 2016].
Shyamsunder, A., A. Pollack and D. Travis (2015), *India Inc.: From Intention to Impact*, Catalyst. Available from: http://www.catalyst.org/system/files/india_inc._from_intention_to_impact.pdf [Accessed 2 August 2016].
Sims, C. and M. Hirudayaraj (2016), 'The impact of colorism on the career aspirations and career opportunities of women in India', *Advances in Developing Human Resources*, **18** (1), no. 1, 38–53.
Sinha, J.B.P. (1984), 'A model of effective leadership styles in India', *International Studies of Management & Organization*, **14** (2–3), 86–98.
Soble, J. (2016), 'Fukushima keeps fighting radioactive tide 5 years after disaster', *The New York Times*, March 10. Available from: https://nyti.ms/1QPcNND [Accessed 19 July 2016].

Social Mobility and Child Poverty Commission (2015), 'State of the nation 2015: Social mobility and child poverty in Great Britain', London: Social Mobility and Child Poverty Commission, December. Web ISBN: 9781474125642. Available from: https://www.gov.uk/government/uploads/system/uploads/attachment_data/file/485926/State_of_the_nation_2015__social_mobility_and_child_poverty_in_Great_Britain.pdf [Accessed 19 September 2016].

Spencer, S. (2014), *Women in Business: Developing Candidates for Senior Executive Roles*. Available from: https://www.spencerstuart.com/~/media/PDF%20Files/Research%20and%20Insight%20PDFs/wib-web_Aug2014-001.pdf [Accessed 22 June 2016].

Stern, J. (2016), 'Mission Journal: Rise in journalist arrests tarnishes Jordan's image as reformist', New York: Committee to Protect Journalists, March 22. Available from: https://cpj.org/x/67b1 [Accessed 7 January 2017].

Stern, S. (2015), 'Women face a maze, not a glass ceiling', *Financial Times*, March 18. Available from: https://www.ft.com/content/e2892610-c95d-11e4-a2d9-00144feab7de [Accessed 11 November 2016].

Stone, J. (2015), 'This is what gender inequality in Britain looks like in charts', *The Independent*, July 14. Available from: http://www.independent.co.uk/news/uk/politics/this-is-what-gender-inequality-in-britain-looks-like-in-charts-10386937.html [Accessed 25 October 2016].

Subhalakshmi, G. (2012), 'Impact of globalization on women workers in India', Washington, DC: International Models Project for Women's Rights, June 6. Available from: http://www.impowr.org/journal/impact-globalization-women-workers-india [Accessed 17 September 2016].

Surie, M.D. (2016), 'Where are India's working women?', Washington, DC: The Asia Foundation, March 19. Available from: http://asiafoundation.org/2016/03/09/where-are-indias-working-women/ [Accessed 17 September 2016].

Sweeney, P. (2011), 'How women are redefining leadership,' *Printing Industries of America, The Magazine*, **3** (1), 60.

Teijin (2014), 'The 8th stakeholder dialogue: True diversity – The next step in the advancement of female employees', *Teijin CSR Report 2014*, 14-20. Tokyo: Teijin Limited. Available from: http://www.teijin.com/csr/report/pdf/csr_14_en_04.pdf [Accessed 17 February 2017].

The Times of India (Online) (2014), 'Gender diversity a mindset battle in the corporate world India business', August 12. Available from: http://timesofindia.indiatimes.com/business/india-business/Gender-diversity-a-mindset-battle-in-the-corporate-world/articleshow/40086984.cms [Accessed 16 September 2016].

'The world needs women leaders' (2008), *Strategic Direction*, **24** (3), 27–9.

Thomson Reuters (2014), 'Most dangerous transport systems for women', Thomson Reuters Foundation News, October 29. Available from: http://news.trust.org/spotlight/most-dangerous-transport-systems-for-women/ [Accessed 26 July 2016].

Thoppil, D.A. (2013), 'After rape, women employees scared to work late', *The Wall Street Journal*, January 4. Available from: http://blogs.wsj.com/indiarealtime/2013/01/04/after-rape-women-employees-scared-to-work-late/ [Accessed 17 September 2016]

Uhl Bien, M., R. Marlon and B. McKelvey (2007), 'Complexity leadership theory: Shifting leadership from the industrial age to the knowledge era', *Leadership Quarterly*, **18** (4), 298–308, reprinted in Ciulla et al., volume 3, 163–98.

UN General Assembly (2105), 'Transforming our world: The 2030 Agenda for Sustainable Development', Resolution 70/1, October 21. Available from: http://www.un.org/ga/search/view_doc.asp?symbol=A/RES/70/1&Lang=E [Accessed 16 June 2016].

UN News Centre (2013), 'Japanese leader advocates "womenomics" in address to UN General Assembly', September 26. Available from: http://www.un.org/apps/news/story.asp?NewsID=46044#.V5ZJU6IYFv8 [Accessed 17 October 2016].

UNDP (2016), 'Shaping the future: How changing demographics can power human development', *Asia-Pacific Human Development Report*, New York: United Nations Development Programme. Available from: http://hdr.undp.org/sites/default/files/rhdr2016-full-report-final-version1.pdf [Accessed 17 September 2016].

United Nations Commission on the Status of Women (2014), *Review and appraisal of the implementation of the Beijing Declaration and Platform for Action and the outcomes of the twenty-third special session of the General Assembly*, December 15, Report no. E/CN.6/2015/3. Available from: http://www.unwomen.org/~/media/headquarters/attachments/sections/csw/59/ecn620153.pdf [Accessed 16 June 2016].

United Nations Development Programme (2012), 'Gender equality and women's empowerment in public administration: Jordan case study', New York: United Nations Development Programme. Available from: http://www.undp.org/content/dam/undp/library/Democratic%20Governance/Women-s%20Empowerment/Jordan Final%20-%20HiRes.pdf [Accessed 3 October 2016].

United Nations Development Programme (2015), *Human Development Report 2015*, New York: United Nations Development Programme. Available from: http://hdr.undp.org/sites/default/files/2015_human_development_report.pdf [Accessed 17 September 2016].

United Nations Secretary-General (2015), *Summary Report: The Beijing Declaration and Platform for Action Turns 20*, New York: UN Women, March. E/CN.6/2015/3. Available from: http://www.unwomen.org/en/digital-library/publications/2015/02/beijing-synthesis-report [Accessed 14 June 2016].

USAID (2016), 'Jordan: Gender equality and female empowerment', USAID, September 28. Available from: https://www.usaid.gov/jordan/gender-equality-womens-empowerment [Accessed 3 October 2016].

Vanderkam, L. (2016), 'The busy person's lies', *The New York Times*, May 13. Available from: http://nyti.ms/24POms3 [Accessed 19 September 2016].

Vinnicombe, S., E. Doldor and C. Turner (2014), *The Female FTSE Board Report 2014*, Cranfield International Centre for Women Leaders. Available from: http://www.som.cranfield.ac.uk/som/p3012/Research/Research-Centres/Cranfield-International-Centre-for-Women-Leaders/Reports [Accessed 22 June 2016].

Vinnicombe S., E. Doldor, R. Sealy, P. Pryce and C. Turner (2015), *The Female FTSE Board Report 2015*, Cranfield International Centre for Women Leaders. Available from: http://www.som.cranfield.ac.uk/som/p3012/Research/Research-Centres/Cranfield-International-Centre-for-Women-Leaders/Reports [Accessed 22 June 2016].

Vinsrygg, K. (2015), 'Believing in being a leader is key to becoming a leader', Speech given at WIN Conference 2015, Rome. Available from: http://www.egonzehnder.com/files/win_2015_speech_karoline_vinsrygg.pdf [Accessed 18 November 2016].

Wang, J. and G.N. McLean (2016), 'Promoting diversity in India: Where do we go from here?', *Advances in Developing Human Resources*, **18** (1), 102–13.

Wells, A.G. (2015), 'Advancing women's empowerment: A shared vision for the United States and Jordan', Address at University of Jordan, March 16. Available from: https://jo.usembassy.gov/advancing-womens-empowerment-a-shared-vision-for-the-united-states-and-jordan/ [Accessed 16 October 2016].

Werhane, P. (2007), 'Women leaders in a globalized world', *Journal of Business Ethics*, **74** (4), 425–35, reprinted in Ciulla et al., volume 3, 3–20.

Werhane, P. and M. Painter-Morland (eds) (2011), *Leadership, Gender, and Organization*, Dordrecht, Netherlands: Springer.

Werhane, P.H., J. Mead, A. Saito, D. Koehn and R. Wolfe (2010a), 'Snow Brand Milk Products (A): Assessing the possibility for revitalization', Case E-0347. Charlottesville, VA: Darden Publishing.

Werhane, P.H., J. Mead, D. Koehn, A. Saito and R. Wolfe (2010b), 'Snow Brand Milk Products (B): Reform and revitalization efforts', Case E-0348. Charlottesville, VA: Darden Publishing.

Werhane, P.H., J. Mead, D. Koehn, A. Saito and R. Wolfe (2010c), 'Snow Brand Milk Products (C): 2009 – Remaining challenges', Case E-0349. Charlottesville, VA: Darden Publishing.

Werhane, P., M. Posig, L. Gundry, L. Ofstein and E. Powell (2007), *Women in Business*, Westport, CT: Praeger.

Workman, L. (2015), 'How outdated stereotypes about British accents reinforce the class ceiling', *The Conversation*, United Kingdom edition, June 30. Available from: http://theconversation.com/how-outdated-stereotypes-about-british-accents-reinforce-the-class-ceiling-43683 [Accessed 11 November 2016].

World Bank (2012), *2012 World Development Report on Gender Equality and Development*, Washington, DC: World Bank. Available from: http://go.worldbank.org/0BP8VT4OE0 [Accessed 16 June 2016].

World Bank (2013), 'Economic participation, agency and access to justice in Jordan', World Bank Report No: ACS5158, July. Available from: http://documents.worldbank.org/curated/en/503361468038992583/Country-gender-assessment-economic-participation-agency-and-access-to-justice-in-Jordan [Accessed 16 October 2016].

World Bank (2014a), *Gender at Work: A Companion to the World Development Report on Jobs*. Washington, DC: World Bank. Available from: https://openknowledge.worldbank.org/handle/10986/17121 [Accessed 16 June 2016].

World Bank (2014b), 'Women in Jordan – Limited economic participation and continued inequality', Washington, DC: World Bank, April 17. Available from: http://www.worldbank.org/en/news/feature/2014/04/17/women-in-jordan---limited-economic-participation-and-continued-inequality [Accessed 4 October 2016].

World Bank, 'Population, female (% of total)', Washington, DC: The World Bank Group. Available from: http://data.worldbank.org/indicator/SP.POP.TOTL.FE.ZS?locations=GB [Accessed 18 November 2016].

World Economic Forum (2014), *Closing the Gender Gap in Japan*, Geneva: World Economic Forum. Available from: http://www3.weforum.org/docs/WEF_ClosingGenderGap_Japan_Report_2014.pdf [Accessed 19 July 2016].

World Economic Forum (2015), *Global Gender Gap Report 2015*, Geneva: World Economic Forum. Available from: http://reports.weforum.org/global-gender-gap-report-2015/ [Accessed 14 June 2016].

Zubaidi, F.R., N.S. Mehdi Al-Sammerai and F. Ahmad (2011), 'An overview on women's leadership issues in Jordan', *Journal of Politics and Law*, **4** (2), 67–73.

Index

Abichandani, Y. 15, 16, 18, 19
Adler, N.J. ix, 9, 156
Adwan, Mohammad 86
Aflatoun International 23, 24
Alafat, Terrie (Chartered Institute of Housing) 113–23, 154, 155
  leadership style 123
  story 113–22
Al Ghad newspaper 87–91
Al Nashmeyat initiative 85
Al-Zoubi, A.F. 81, 82
Anan, Hisa (Megmilk Snow Brand Co., Ltd.) 52–5
  leadership style 54–5
  story 52–4
Arab International Women's Forum (AIWF) 84
Arora, P. 46n1
Asahi Chemical Company 70
Asahi Kasei Corporation 73n5
ASEAN countries 2
Asia Foundation report 18
Asian Women's Human Rights Council 38
Asia Pacific Association of Surgical Tissue Banking (APASTB) 30, 31
Asia-Pacific tissue bank community 30
Asking, We Walk: The South as a New Political Imaginary 40
Auslin, M. 51
Azzeh, L. 86

Bakshi, S.K. 15
Barcucci, V. 82
Basirov, Olga x

Bass, B. 5, 6
Batra, R. 18
Beasley, A.L. 11
Beijing Platform for Action (BPfA) 1
Big Bang 137, 144n1
Billimoria, Jeroo (social entrepreneur) 20–24, 154, 155
  leadership styles 23
  in the Netherlands 21–3
  story 20–23
Biolab 84
Black, C. 51
Burger King 73n3
Burns, J.M. 5, 6

Caliper Research & Development Department 9
Carter, M.N. 18
Catalyst 49–5, 107
Centre of Informal Education and Development Studies (CIEDS) 37
Chartered Institute of Housing 113–23
Child and Youth Finance International (CYFI) 22, 24n4
Child Helpline International 21
Childline India 21, 24n2
City of London 136n1, 144n2
Ciulla, J. 3, 4, 9, 10
Club of Rome 151, 152n4
Cohen, C. 153
Collier, J. 10
Collins, J.C. 15, 16, 18–19
colorism 17
complex adaptive systems 9

Conger, J. 3
consumer affairs agency 53
Consumer Cooperative Association in Tokyo 52
consumer rights articulation 53
Cordes, S. 81–6
corporate social responsibility (CSR) 64, 66–7, 68, 85
CSR Planning Office, Teijin Ltd. 66–7
cultural capital 110
cytomegalovirus (CMV) 148, 149, 152n1

Dartmouth College 113–14, 123n2
Davidson, L. 51
Davies, Lord 108
Debusscher, P. 1
De Valk, P. 108, 112
Dobbs, R. 15, 16
Dutt, K.G. 46n1

Eagly, A.H. 6
Eagly, Robin 5
EcoBalance 67
economic capital 110
Eisner, S. 6–8
El Taller International 39
Esteban, R. 10
ExCo 128, 129, 136

Fackler, M. 55n2
Fawcett Society report 107
female leadership development 112
fierce price war 73n3
Folke Bernadotte Academy (FBA) 102, 103n2
Freedom House 83
Frère, Vincente 36
Freud, Sigmund 3
Friedman, S. 112n1
FTSE 100 companies 107, 108, 110, 153
Fukushima Daiichi nuclear plant 54, 55n2

Gajiwala, Astrid Lobo (Tata Memorial Hospital Tissue Bank) 25–33, 154
leadership style 33
story 25–33
Gallaher Group plc 136n2
Gandhi, Mohandas Karamchand 6, 38, 41n3
Gandhism 40, 41n3
Gator(s), University of Florida 69, 73n2
gender 7–8
gender equality 107
gender pay gap 107
Gender Sensitization Project 84
gender stereotypes 16, 76
gender wage gap 54
Ghazal, M. 90
Ghunaimat, J. (*Al Ghad* newspaper) 87–91, 154
leadership style 90–91
postscript 90
story 87–9
Gilligan, C. 3–5, 55
global leadership ix
Global South *see* South
godown 27, 34n3
Government Equalities Office 111
Grand Metropolitan PLC 73n4
Grant Thornton International Ltd. 2
Greenberg, H.M. 8
Greenleaf, R. 7

Hassan, Reem Abu (attorney at law) x, 92–7, 154
leadership style 97
story 92–7
hierarchical leadership model 10
Hirudayaraj, M. 17
histochemistry 26, 34n1
Hiwasa, Nobuko (Megmilk Snow Brand Co., Ltd.) x, 53, 56–65
leadership style 65
story 56–64
homelessness 118, 117

Index 183

Iinuma, A. 51
Imam, Noor 85
impressionism 126
Indian women leaders
　Billimoria, Jeroo 20–24
　Gajiwala, Astrid Lobo 25–33
　Kumar, Corinne 35–42
　Sujata, Sharma 43–6
informal sector employment 15
Institute of Leadership and
　Management (ILM) 108, 109
International Atomic Energy
　Agency (IAEA) project 27,
　29
International Finance Corporation
　81, 83
International Labour Organization
　(ILO) 1
International Organization for
　Standardization (ISO) 34n4
investor relations (IR) 128
Illich, Ivan 37–8, 41

jaha 93
Jamieson, P. 6
Japanese Consumers' Co-operative
　Union (JCCU) 60, 61
Japanese women leaders
　Anan, Hisa 52–5
　Hiwasa, Nobuko 56–65
　Kurose, Yukako 66–7
　Nagata, Ryoko 68–73
　Yoshida, Mieko 74–7
Japan Tobacco, Inc. 64, 68–73
Jenkins, Claire (Sports Direct
　International plc) 124–36,
　154, 155
　leadership style 136
　story 124–36
Johannesen-Schmidt, M.C. 6
Johnson, Rebecca 42n6
joint family system 15
Jordan Ahli Bank 84–6
Jordan Business 85
Jordanian women leaders

Ghunaimat, Jumana 87–91
Hassan, Reem Abu 92–7
Shamroukh, Nadia 98–103
Jordanian Women's Union (JWU)
　98–103
Jordan Press Association 90
Jordan Times 86

Kanungo, R. 3
Kellaway, L. 156
Kennedy, John F. 53, 55n1
Kumar, Corinne (World Courts of
　Women) 35–42, 154
　four-volume anthology 40
　leadership style 41
　story 35–41
　in Tunisia 39, 40
Kurmanath, K.V. 18
Kurose, Yukako (CSR Planning
　Office, Teijin Ltd.) 66–7
　leadership style 67
　story 66–7
KVINFO 84, 85

labor laws 83
Lamb, H. 109
The Lancet statement 148
leader-follower relationships 5
Leningrad 123n1
Lewis, G. 156
Lewis, L. 51
Lichner, Jeannette 8
Lord Davies of Abersoch, Steering
　Committee 107, 108, 110,
　111
loyalty card scheme 126
lunch club 126

Madhav, R. 16
Mavin, S. 109, 110
McDonald, M. 55n2
McKinsey Global Institute (MGI)
　15
McLane, Charles 114
McLean, G.N. 16

Megmilk Snow Brand Co., Ltd. 52–5, 64
Meiji era 56
Meiji Restoration 66n1
MelJol 21, 24n1
Middle East and North Africa Businesswomen's Network (MENA BWN) 84
Millennium Development Goals (MDGs) 1, 81
Monga, Manjit x
Mryyan, N. 82
Murtaugh, Maurine x

Nagata, Ryoko (Japan Tobacco Inc.) 68–73
  leadership style 73
  story 68–73
Nag, D. 17
National Council of Family Affairs (NCFA) 92, 94
National Liaison Committee of Consumer Organizations 65n2
Nemoto, K. 49
Nisshin Seifun Group Inc. 74–77
non-violent civil disobedience 41n3
North American women business leaders ix
The Nuffield Council on Bioethics 150, 152n2
Nyerere, Julius 42n5

O'Connell, Francesca Raleigh (SculptureLondon) 137–45, 154
  leadership style 144
  story 137–44
Olchawski, J. 107
organizational decision-making 5

Painter-Morland, M. 10
Peckham, Catherine (University College London) 146–52, 154
  leadership style 152
  story 146–52

Peeling, Rosanna x
Personal Status Law, Jordan 99
Pleas, Nicola x
pluralism 37
poverty rates 54
POWERful Women (PfW) 111
PricewaterhouseCoopers 111

rainmaker 142, 144n4
recruitment decision making 107
Reio, T.G. 18
resilience 122
Reuters 17
Rexam plc 136n4
right to be heard 55n1
right to be informed 55n1
right to choose 55n1
right to safety 55n1
Roberts, G.S. 50
Rosener, J.B. 5, 6
Royal Borough of Kensington and Chelsea 113, 115–16, 123n3
RSA Group report 112
Rustagi, P. 16

SAMENA Telecommunications Council 85
Sankaran, K. 16
Schermerhorn, J. 7
Scullin, Caroline x
Sealy, R. 109, 153
servant-leadership orientation 7
Shamroukh, Nadia (Jordanian Women's Union) 98–103
  leadership style 102
  story 98–102
Shodanren 61, 65n2
Shogunate period 65n1
Shriberg A. 3
Shriberg, D. 3
Shyamsunder, A. 18
Sims, C. 17
small and medium size enterprises (SMEs) 82

Index

Snow Brand Milk Products Co., Ltd. (SBM) 56, 61, 63
Soble, J. 55n2
Social Mobility and Child Poverty Commission 110, 112n1
South 38, 40, 41n2
Sports Direct International plc 124–36
Stern, S. 108
Sujata, Sharma (Tapan Rehabilitation Society) 43–6, 154, 155
  leadership style 46–7
  story 43–5
Surie, M.D. 16–18
Sweeney, P.J. 8

Tapan Rehabilitation Society 43–6
Tata Institute of Social Sciences (TISS) 20
Tata Memorial Hospital Tissue Bank 25–33
Teijin 67
tissue banking 25–30
Tokyo Consumers' Co-operative Union (TCCU) 61
Tokyo Woman's Christian University (TWCU) 58
trait theory 3
transactional leader 5
transformational leadership 6
Transplantation of Human Organs Act 31
Tutu, Archbishop Desmond 39

Uhl-Bien, M. 9, 10
Ujamaa 40, 42n5
Umniah Mobile Company 84
United Kingdom women leaders
  Alafat, Terrie 113–23

Jenkins, Claire 124–36
O'Connell, Francesca Raleigh 137–45
Peckham, Catherine 146–52
United Nations Development Programme (UNDP) 18, 81–3
University College London 146–52
UN News Centre 51
UN women 103n1
US-Japan security treaty 59

viva 26, 34n2

Wang, J. 16
Werhane, P.H. ix, 5, 10, 61–4
The Wolf of Wall Street 142, 144n5
women
  challenges for 8–9
  global leadership 9–10
  and leadership 2–10
  leadership styles 5–6
  vs. men 3–4
  systems thinking 9–10
  women's advancement 1, 84
  women's empowerment 1, 25, 38, 84–5, 92
Workman, L. 112n1
World Bank 82, 83
World Courts of Women 35–42
World Economic Forum 51
Wykehamists 141, 144n3

Yoshida, Mieko (Nisshin Seifun Group Inc.) 74–77
  leadership style 77
  story 74–77
Young Arab Women Leaders 84

Zapatismo 40, 41n4
Zehnder, Egon 110